The Educator's
ATLAS

The Educator's ATLAS

Your Roadmap to Engagement

Weston Kieschnick

ConnectEDD Publishing
Hanover, Pennsylvania

This publication is available at discount pricing when purchased in quantity for educational purposes, promotions, or fundraisers. For inquiries and details, contact the publisher at
info@connecteddpublishing.com

Published by ConnectEDD Publishing LLC
Hanover, PA
www.connecteddpublishing.com

Cover Design: Kheila Dunkerly

The Educator's ATLAS/Weston Kieschnick. —1st ed.
Paperback ISBN 978-1-7361996-8-8

Praise for *The Educator's ATLAS*

"Kieschnick had my attention at 'Prioritize student engagement above every other thing.' I was leaning in his direction when he counsels readers to 'imbue classrooms with positivity.' I was looking for the dotted line when he not only pointed to the futility of a curriculum of coverage but when he also provided sensible alternatives, and I was looking for a pen to sign on as he reminds us that our students are human beings whose emotions must be engaged at least as much as their cognition for learning to happen and when I understood that he was equally respectful of teacher needs as of the needs of the young people they teach. What finalized the deal for me, however, was the moment that I realized he has not only developed a practical framework for teachers to use in engaging learners but that he has actually written a highly engaging book by applying every element of the framework for engagement that he commends!"

    —Carol Ann Tomlinson, Ed.D. | William Clay Parrish, Jr.
    Professor Emeritus School of Education & Human
    Development University of Virginia

"Weston hit it out of the park with *ATLAS*, and it is top on my list of recommended books for all educators! Weston has a way of turning theory into practice with his witty stories and powerful anecdotes. Wherever you are on your education journey, there are so many ideas, examples, and practical applications that can be implemented for all educators!"

    —Nathan Lang-Raad, Ed.D. | Speaker and Author

"Weston is a master of turning ambiguous topics like 'engagement' into approachable and empowering actions ANY educator can apply. I wish I had this book when I first started teaching, but it's just as powerful of a resource for a veteran educator. At a time when educators everywhere are feeling the inefficacy of engaging modern learners, *ATLAS* is a must read to guide us to confidence and competence."

—Chase Mielke | Instructional Coach, Speaker, and best-selling
author of *The Burnout Cure: Learning to Love Teaching Again*

"I thought Weston's first two books were absolute game changers in the education space, and then *ATLAS* came along, and he's absolutely raised the bar. With a blend of humor, research, stories, real life application and engagement strategies that just work, Wes has brought it all together in *ALTAS*. Kids remember what they learn when they're engaged in their learning, not entertained, but engaged. With years and years of experience doing the teaching himself and teaching others how to implement these ideas, you're going to read this book and right away ramp up the engagement in your classroom! This is a MUST read and a MUST purchase for all teachers, coaches, administrators, and anyone working with kids!"

—Adam Welcome | Educator, Author, Speaker, Podcaster

"*The Educator's ATLAS* by Weston Kieschnick is a must-read for educators looking to understand the puzzle of student engagement and bring about impactful changes in the classroom. Building on his foundation for designing learning experiences and the importance of relationships from his first two books, *Bold School* and *Breaking Bold*, Weston now shares the *ATLAS* model for student engagement. The *ATLAS* model is brilliant and can be implemented in any classroom. Through decades of personal and professional learning experiences, Weston has designed the *ATLAS* model to guide educators as they connect with learners to create authentic experiences to help them thrive and truly engage in learning. Weston's commitment to and passion for helping and inspiring educators to do what's best and whatever it takes for all students is contagious. Each of the personal stories are supported with research, solid strategies, and best practices to help educators improve instruction and truly understand student engagement and its impact on learning. I have followed Weston's work for several years and highly recommend *The Educator's ATLAS*. If you know Weston, you know that in this book, you will find humor, insight, inspiration, and so much more. The authentic and relatable stories will empower you to take risks and bring amazing transformations to your classroom every day!"

—Rachelle Dené Poth | Educator, Author, Consultant, Attorney

"Weston Kieschnick has done it again! On the heels of two best-selling books, he dives into the ever-so-important concept of engaging learners at the perfect time. His *ATLAS* model lays out concrete steps that any educator can implement immediately to reach all types of students to immerse them in lessons of all types. Using a mix of humor, research, and practical examples, you will be hard pressed to put this book down."

—Eric Sheninger, Keynote speaker and best-selling author

"Wes has an exceptional ability to take best practices and convert them into steps that are easy to get behind. *The Educator's ATLAS* is no exception. *ATLAS* allows educators to methodically strengthen their ability to create higher degrees of student engagement through practical steps that lead to immediate outcomes."

—Anthony Kim | author of *The New School Rules* and founder of Education Elements

"A book about engaging learners should engage the reader from page 1. *ATLAS* did exactly that and it was only the beginning. Kieschnick does a masterful job of engaging the reader and making sure the content is not only relatable, but also easy for the leader to implement. The *ATLAS* model is not only explained, but also used in the text to ensure engagement throughout. As a school leader, I found myself thinking about how I am going to use it with our staff. As someone who works with school leaders, I found myself thinking about how I engage people in their own professional growth. The research supports the process, and the stories keep you hooked. Absolutely exceptional."

—Joe Sanfelippo | Superintendent, Speaker, Author

"If we want students to learn, we must authentically engage them in relevant and meaningful learning. Engagement matters! Weston Kieschnick provides readers with a BOLD and accessible framework in *ATLAS* that helps to engage students and teachers in learning that inspires the genius and sparks curiosity in all students."

—Dr. Tyrone Howard | Professor of Education, UCLA Graduate School of Education

"As educators, we want to do what is best for our students. We want to skyrocket the learning so we can stand proud and celebrate the success of our students. We want to engage them in a way that breaks through their short attention span to create moments of exponential learning. Sounds like a dream? Don't fret because Weston has made it possible as he shares a direct path and powerful tidbits, along with a pinch of humor, to help YOU be successful engaging YOUR students. Buckle up and get going!"

—LaVonna Roth Speaker | Author & Chief Illuminator for Ignite Your S.H.I.N.E.®

"Weston Kieschnick's *ATLAS* is a must-read book for all educators! Weston's practice of using wit and stories drive the messages home. This is the blueprint for successful teaching and engagement with students."

—Elizabeth Hamilton-Guarino | bestselling author of *The Change Guidebook* and CEO of The Best Ever You Network

"For too long, we have relied on school improvement efforts focused on content and assessments as drivers for improvement. Especially now, in the wake of the learning disruptions that COVID-19 brought, putting student engagement at the center of our efforts must be our priority. While there might be broad agreement about the importance of engagement, there is decidedly less about the actions classroom practitioners can take to create meaningful and authentic learning environments. In *The Educator's ATLAS*, Weston Kieschnick lays out a clear framework and plan of action for doing just that. It is my sincere hope that this model is widely used in our country, and through it we help our students fall in love again with learning and school."

> —Jason E. Glass, Ed.D. | Commissioner, Kentucky Department of Education

"I was captivated by this book from start to finish! Student engagement doesn't have to be something elusive and unreachable. In *The Educator's ATLAS*, Kieschnick describes a clear and compelling framework, grounded in research and tested in practice, that will help make learning irresistible in your classroom. Follow his process, have fun with it, and you'll connect your students to learning in ways you've only imagined."

> —David Geurin | Educator, Speaker, Author of *Future Driven: Will Your Student Thrive in an Unpredictable World?*

"*ATLAS* is a brilliant call to action that serves as a roadmap to boldly engage students. With the goal of putting teachers back in the driver's seat of student engagement, Weston inspires educators to deeply understand their students, the art of learning, and to leverage possibilities using the ATLAS model. As someone passionate about education and an advocate for teachers, Weston genuinely cares about working alongside educators to create experiences that foster memorable learning for students and brings joy to schools. In *ATLAS*, Weston provides a compelling, yet practical guide for educators that should be a key-stone in your school's professional learning library."

—Elisabeth Bostwick | multi-award winning educator, author of *Take the L.E.A.P. Ignite a Culture of Innovation*, and innovative teaching and learning coach

"Guess what? We don't learn much if we're not interested. Wes is a master storyteller who vigorously reminds us that we ignore learner apathy at our peril. In this spellbinding book, Wes uses his trademark energy and humor to share his easily-implemented *ATLAS* framework for enhanced student engagement and understanding. This book is not about entertaining kids; it's about creating active, meaningful learning opportunities for our children. I was hooked within the first few pages, and you will be too. We must do better by all of the bored, disengaged students in our schools. This book will help."

—Dr. Scott McLeod | Professor of Educational Leadership, University of Colorado Denver; Founding Director, CASTLE

Dedication

For Everett and Charlotte
Be Curious.
Participate.
Persevere.

Table of Contents

Foreword

by Steve Arrowood

Weston's creative partner and engagement coach

I knew Weston before it meant anything to say you knew Weston. Saying you knew Weston used to be exactly like saying, "I know table salt." Nobody cared and most people would reply, "What does that mean?"

If that sounds harsh, buckle up.

I met Weston at Stanford University. It was his first year in a camp counselor teaching position at an academic summer program for high schoolers. My job was to train the staff in instruction and engagement.

No joke, upon seeing Weston for the first time, my initial thought was, "Who's the dude from the American Eagle catalog, and is he going to model some cargo shorts?" He also appeared to have a stakeholder-level interest in sleeveless shirts.

When he started to do his first instructional practice presentation, it looked like he was working off a public speaking checklist he scribbled on a napkin while his mom drove him there:

Step 1: Talk at the speed of an auctioneer!

Step 2: Flail arms nonsensically!

Step 3: Mention multiple times my profuse sweat to make people comfortable with my moistness!

Yikes.

Not to toot my own horn, but I'd studied performance psychology with US Olympic coaches, won my share of awards for speaking and presentation, trained under educational luminaries who transformed teaching and learning as we know it—and now I'm supposed to coach up Mr. Manscape?

One unassuming afternoon a few days into the program, I was walking across campus and came across Weston, sitting in a circle with a dozen high school students. Taking a deep breath to fill myself with the serenity that would enable me to observe his work, I casually leaned against a nearby wall to see how things were going—and I saw the unexpected.

He was doing something that's quite easy to overlook, but it's something that the most engaging presenters and instructors do. It was something I first encountered when studying group dynamics under Harvard University's Head of Voice and Speech: He completely committed himself to each and every moment with the students.

He asked questions. He was a focused listener. He fluidly shifted his acuity between individuals and the larger group. People talk a lot about how important "presence" is, but far more impactful is the ability to be *present* with people. And only one of them leads to the other.

My work with Weston that summer became about channeling his raw enthusiasm into intentionally engaging instruction and presentation. Every day we lived the mantra: *Learning is the message. Engagement is the volume. If it ain't turned up, they ain't gonna learn.*

Fast forward twenty some years, and I'm still working with this guy. It's not because he needs a lot of help to be good anymore. The truth is, we still work together because Weston genuinely believes in being better today than he was yesterday. The difference between an Olympian's learning mindset and a typical one is that as an Olympian's skill improves, they don't want *less* coaching—they want more.

And as far as his purpose goes, his *why* for doing this work—having trained thousands of people, I know that many are not in it for their audiences—they say they are, they think they are, but they're really there because they want to look good. Weston helps people feel that they're the reason he's there instead of the other way around. Even his thrashing gesticulations don't distract from his sincerity.

As his thought partner for a couple decades, he's solicited my input on honing his *ATLAS* model, which is a powerful engagement framework for teachers and students. I've seen educators in his sessions not only gain a clear sense of how to actualize *ATLAS* in their practice but also leave feeling inspired and empowered.

And for those of you interested in the behind the scenes, Weston uses *ATLAS* himself to craft his singular keynotes. It's through this model that he deliberately achieves precisely what he wants to achieve: to harness and sustain audience engagement so he can empower them to become engagement pros themselves.

Two decades after our first meeting, I can confidently say that Weston has graduated from his camp counselor years. I fully expect that someday he'll invite me to the retirement home for porridge and prune juice so we can discuss how to properly integrate the phrase "excessive chest hair" for an upcoming keynote to the AARP.

In the meantime, trust me when I say: You're in great hands with Weston. You and your students will be in great hands with the *ATLAS* model. It's lighting up classrooms around the globe. Yours can be next.

Introduction

To mention the Covid-19 pandemic or not to mention the Covid-19 pandemic in a book about student engagement, that is the question.

I started writing this book over the summer of 2021, when district and school leaders were huddling in Zoom-tile formation to determine the best path forward for the 2021-2022 school year. Complicated schedules negotiating dozens of student pods on constant rotation between in-person and online school days were drafted. Maze-like flow charts were stitched together to lay out provisions for all kinds of "if/then" Covid possibilities. Multiple contingencies were conceived. And then, on a wing and a prayer, these complicated plans were put into motion.

By the time I completed this book in the spring of 2022, it was clear that pretty much every school out there pulled it off—you got and kept kids in school with only brief returns to online learning. Thank you, educators. That was no small feat. You've not had it easy in recent years. But by the start of the 2021-2022 school year, the ingenuity, commitment, and adaptability of our educators and school structure was clear. What would take a little more time to manifest in full was a serious crisis of student engagement.

In a post-pandemic world, student engagement is the topic I'm hearing discussed most often in central offices and school meeting rooms. And rightly so. The pandemic laid bare the problem and urgency of engagement. That said, here is my reluctance in mentioning—let alone starting with—the pandemic in a book about student engagement: Student engagement, as a priority in schools, is timeless. I don't care what historical epoch we're in, what conversations might be trending in schools, or what technology rules the day, student engagement has always been and will always be vital to successful learning and life outcomes.

The pandemic has left no shortage of "more than ever" statements in its wake, most of which border on hyperbole or lose the plot. The latter is true when it comes to engagement. I shudder a bit when I hear people say, "Student engagement matters more than ever." Like so many priorities, personal and professional, that may have fallen by the wayside in our overly busy pre-pandemic lives, the most meaningful came into clearer focus due to the pandemic. It's not that these things matter more now, it's that we let other things distract us from their preeminence. To suggest that the most important things weren't *always* the most important things keeps them vulnerable to falling by the wayside once again in the future. The pandemic has provided an opportunity to redouble our commitment to what has always mattered most.

The same goes for student engagement. Much has been written about pandemic learning loss. I don't want to belabor that point here, and frankly only so much good can come from drowning in the depressing for too long. I will simply say that it is because of learning loss's stark realities that many are now uttering, "Student engagement matters more than ever."

I take issue with the implication that engagement used to be less critical, not just before the pandemic but at any previous moment in the history of school. In terms of students' success in school and their lives beyond it, as well as our success as educators, student engagement has *always* mattered more than most other things. But we let other, far less important and urgent things supplant it. We let tools, practices, concepts, or "silver bullets" that offer little in the way of valuable returns trump the one thing that is linked to exponentially improved student outcomes, both short- and long-term and across multiple categories: student engagement.

I'd like to suggest another angle: It's not that engagement matters more than ever. It's that, due to the pandemic and all it has wrought, teachers have every reason to prioritize student engagement above every other thing. Once and for all.

> Due to the pandemic and all it has wrought, teachers have every reason to prioritize student engagement above every other thing.

In fact, we have a duty to do so, and we should feel entitled and affirmed in demanding it. If we tell ourselves anything less, if we allow ourselves to backslide into thinking student engagement is a lesser priority than it is, then once again we will inevitably let it fall by the wayside, with students paying the heaviest price.

You'll learn in these pages that engagement has always been a focus of my teaching practice. You'll see how I constructed the *ATLAS* model of student engagement decades ago and have been obsessively refining it since. But it wasn't until this moment—this opportunity—that I decided to put pen to paper and share it broadly–because I know this method works and can help teachers regain control of their classrooms and their students' success. The model is built on the backs of the greats—in categories from teaching to coaching, speaking to storytelling—who taught me that heady feeling of engagement so exciting and enthralling that tunnel vision takes over and everything else turns to blur. And it's built on the backs of those who taught me how to elicit this kind of engagement within others. *ATLAS* is time tested and has been workshopped and improved in classrooms across the globe.

Teachers: This is your moment. When I travel across the world talking to educators, nine times out of ten, you lead with how much you love students. How much joy it gives you to see them grow and learn. What an honor it is to serve as one of their guides, a person who has the power to positively influence how they feel about themselves and their potential. And the next statement is how maddening it is when you are forced to focus on things that don't matter and ultimately come at the expense of the best student outcomes possible. You know what's best for your students: teaching that engages each of them, every day. You've always known this to be true, you've always been frustrated when others try to steer you elsewhere. Today—whatever day this might be, in whatever year you might be reading this book—is the day to say enough is enough.

It's time to put student engagement first. It's time we finally hold it as our most important objective in our classrooms, across our schools, and throughout our districts. If not today, when? If not you, who?

I invite you to join me in a new-found conviction and commitment to pushing back on distractions that pull us away from focusing on student engagement. Speak up for student engagement as the critical priority of our post-pandemic teaching world. We can seize the opportunity the pandemic created

> It's time to put student engagement first. It's time we finally hold it as our most important objective in our classrooms, across our schools, and throughout our districts. If not today, when? If not you, who?

to fight for what's right. And as you do, remind people that student engagement always mattered most and must continue to matter most, no matter what might be coming down the pipeline. When it comes to making and proving your case, trust that the *ATLAS* model is our ace in the hole. When you follow this model, all other priorities will much more readily, even often naturally, fall into place. The *ATLAS* model is the goal that, when achieved, enables all other instructional and learning goals to become much more accessible. It is the goal that will render the best possible outcomes for all students.

Brass Tacks

I wrote this book to be concise and straightforward. I don't want to waste your time, as I know you have little to spare. The model is also not complicated, and I wanted the length of the chapters and book to reflect that.

ATLAS is an acronym for the five components that will allow you to plan every moment of a class optimized for engagement—where every decision is designed to squeeze the most engagement from every moment and every student. *ATLAS* stands for: **A**ttention, **T**ransition, **L**esson, **A**ctivity, and **S**ummation.

The first two chapters make the case and lay the foundation for the *ATLAS* model. Chapters 3 through 7 each tackle a respective component of *ATLAS*. In Chapter 8, I share a series of *ATLAS* exemplars across grade levels and subject areas so that you can begin to envision with more clarity what *ATLAS* looks like in practice and imagine how you might apply it yourself. And that's it. Short. Simple. To the point. And ready to use.

Merging the *ATLAS* Model with Your Lesson Planning Framework

The *ATLAS* model is not a wholesale replacement of how you approach lesson planning. It's meant to work with what's already working for you. It's designed to augment what you already know, trust, and do best but with an eye on enhanced student engagement.

For those of you who've read my first book, *Bold School: Old School Wisdom + New School Technologies = Blended Learning That Works*, you are familiar with The Bold School Framework for Strategic Blended Learning™. The framework's emphasis is on blended learning. With small adjustments, it can be used for any kind of learning and is just as powerful for analog learning, too. While I won't explain the framework in detail, here's a quick refresh:

The Bold School Framework for Strategic Blended Learning

1 Identify Desired Academic Outcome(s)

2 Select a Goal-Aligned Instructional Strategy That Works

3 Choose Digital Tool

4 Plan Blended Instruction

5 Self-Assess Your Plans and Progress with a Framework

If you use this framework to plan classes, first, thank you. Second, know that the *ATLAS* model can fit right into Step 4, the planning step. The framework and model are not only compatible, but they are also stronger together.

If you don't use the Bold School Framework, first, we're still friends. Second, know that the *ATLAS* model can fit into any larger lesson planning framework you already use. I'm not here to change what already works for you. I'm offering a way to layer what you're already doing with a formula that infuses every instructional decision and every learning moment with engagement.

As you'll soon learn, the *ATLAS* model rests on a new and improved definition of engagement. One that finally clarifies *your* role in student engagement. While, ultimately, all our decisions and learning goals must be about students, learning can't and won't happen without you. You, teachers, must and do hold equal importance in the engagement equation. It's not just that you are *permitted* to bring yourself fully into planning for the most engagement possible, it's that you are *required* to do so. Your teaching skills and pedagogical knowledge are needed. But so, too, is your imagination, your creativity, even your humor and wit. *ATLAS* needs all of *you*, and that's what makes it fun and fulfilling, in addition to effective.

Thank you for showing up fully for your students. They will thank you, too.

CHAPTER 1

Raising the Bar

There's a universal truth in teaching. Even the most seasoned and expert among us experience this truth. No teacher can avoid it. It's an inescapable reality, an inevitability. And that is that in our first years of teaching, we feel like clueless frauds more days than not.

I vividly remember closing the door to my classroom for the first time. The door clicked, and I turned to find thirty teenagers staring me in the face. I remember thinking, *Oh my God. They just left these kids with me. I have no idea what I'm doing!* Many of us have such memories—where we experienced sheer terror that someone allowed *us* to get up in front of children and pretend we actually know how to teach them—seared deep into our brains in the way only trauma can do. Yeah, they taught us all the "important" theories and strategies in school. But theory is exceedingly different from practice, as we all well know. And each of us has battle wounds and humiliating stories to prove it.

Eventually, we begin to figure out this teaching thing. We fall on our faces, and we get back up a little stronger, a little wiser, and a little more resilient. We improve, we collaborate and learn with colleagues. And, magically, one day we wake up and feel like maybe we belong.

No, the learning and growth never end. But the confidence eventually moves outta the red and ever more into the black.

The path to this point, however, is variable. The lucky among us will have a mentor early on who gives us a nugget or insight that can function as a life raft in our first years of teaching. It can give us at least one thing to latch onto and keep from panicking as an entire classroom of equally-horrified children watches us drown in a sea of educational theory and professorial bullshit that professors told us in college would work. (Yes, I'm looking at you, university schools of education). Or at least that's how it feels. Shudder.

For me, my life raft came by way of a mentor named Mark Essay—who was legally required to become an English teacher on account of his last name. I kid, although his last name had to have something to do with his choice to teach English, no? I met Mark at an academic summer camp for high school students, where I'd been hired as camp counselor during two of my summers in college. It was a great opportunity for me to get meaningful experience working with high school kids. And, even more importantly, to see Mark, a master educator, in action. He had an incredible talent for "surprising" students with learning. By which I mean, he almost tricked kids into learning by drawing them in with engaging stories and anecdotes before they were aware that formal learning had even begun. He would often say that some of the best learning happens before kids realize it's even happening.

> Some of the best learning happens before kids realize it's even happening.

One day, the entire staff and all 150 students were congregated in the main meeting hall. Mark walked into the middle of the room. To get everyone's attention, he didn't say, "Quiet down, time to start our discussion on science." Instead, he just launched into a story.

Mark said, "Everyone look down at the ground. Imagine that there's a giant clock face on the center of the floor. You're going to need this visual as I tell you a funny story."

From the 1 o'clock spot of the imaginary clock face, Mark launched into a story about how he was planning to propose to his girlfriend. He had recently gone to the jewelry store, he explained, to look for a gemstone for the engagement ring.

"I found the perfect gem," Mark said. "So, I held it up to inspect it closely under good light." As he said this, Mark held up his hands as though he was holding a giant gemstone. "Everybody, hold up your gems!" All 150 kids and even us staff held up our imaginary gems.

"Oh, there's a spot on it." With an exaggerated and audible "haa haa," Mark blew on his imaginary gem, similar to how we breathe on sunglasses before wiping them clean, and then pretended to wipe off the spot. He cued everyone in the room to do the same. We all blew on our gems, "haa haa," and wiped them clean.

"You'll never believe who walked into the jewelry store at that very moment. My girlfriend! I panicked. Everyone, really quickly, hide your gem! Hide your gem!" he said at a quickening pace. Following his command, everyone put their gems into their pockets.

"Haa no! We can't put gems in our pockets in a jewelry store, we'll look like criminals! We gotta get outta here," Mark said as he jumped to the imaginary 2 o'clock spot on the clock face and launched into a story about his niece.

"My two-year-old niece, she loves balloons. Like, she cannot get enough of balloons. She takes them with her wherever she goes. One day, my sister was bringing my niece over to my place so we could hang out for a bit. When I opened the door, I saw my niece standing there holding, what?"

"Balloons!" The entire room shouted.

"Yes!" Mark said, as he held up imaginary balloons in his right hand. "She's holding two balloons, and she's giggling and saying 'Hee hee hee, balloons! Hee hee hee, balloons!'"

Mark goes on to tell a little story for every hour on the clock face. In each story, there's a distinctly memorable set of words, and there's some sort of body movement or audience refrain that goes along with each to help students remember key items. A few stories in, it occurred to me, *Holy cow, he's teaching us the first twelve elements of the periodic table, their symbol, and their number on the table!* And in a way that was captivating—which was not how the periodic table was taught to me in school. I recall zoning out when my high school teacher lectured on the elements, essentially just listing them.

In Mark's approach, we were given a clever story where "hide your gem"—said really fast—was a mnemonic for *hydrogen*, element number one at the 1 o'clock spot, with an atomic symbol of H. And balloons, told at 2 o'clock, helped us remember element number two, *helium*, with an atomic symbol of "He." And on he went up to *magnesium* at 12 o'clock.

All the students were listening and laughing along as Mark used stories to repeat key information to prime their brains for retention. He had all of us, even all the staff members, hanging on his every word. As a college student who'd begun doing some student teaching, I'd learned how challenging it could be to engage a class of twenty-five students. Mark had managed to engage 150 *teenagers* and all the adults in the room!

After Mark completed his twelve clock-face stories, the students were energized and giving Mark their full attention. From there, he transitioned into a proper class session in which he showed why elements matter and how they impact our daily lives. He engaged them in a session that went far beyond listing a strange collection of symbols and numbers on some table. So much so that, more than twenty years later, I still remember what he taught all of us that day. I suspect nearly everyone who was in that hall does, too.

I loved how Mark surprised students into learning. He was so skilled at using memorable stories, mnemonics, and total physical response (those body movements and gestures) to grab students' attention before the formal learning had even begun. While I was too young and green to grasp how and why Mark was so calculated in plotting learning from start to finish, I gravitated towards his style of teaching, which, refreshingly, began with wonder rather than an audible groan.

I'm fortunate to have met Mark Essay so early in my teaching career. His life raft saved me from sinking in my first teaching job, which was at a public high school in Bermuda. Yes, you read that right. And no, it was not a working vacation. In fact, to date—and after working with teachers and school leaders from every state in America and more than thirty countries around the world—I can tell you that this school in Bermuda is by far the most difficult place I've ever worked. The circumstances of this school were challenging. Bermuda's wealth divide is staggering. The rich are ultra-rich and can send their kids to private school. Meanwhile, the poor live in communities where crime and drug use are prevalent and kids go to public school. I taught at the largest public school on the island. Teacher turnover at this school was high. Student grades were low. And dropping out was commonplace for students across all grade levels.

As you can imagine, student engagement was a constant struggle at this school. The teachers who had stuck around were often worn down, demoralized, and tired. Most were in survival mode; they were not in the mindset of planning the kind of classes that sparked curiosity, elicited participation, and made students want to persevere through challenging work. Leadership was so preoccupied with putting out daily fires that they had little remaining bandwidth to support teachers with learning and successfully applying effective teaching methodologies and instructional strategies. Everyone was stretched thin and, justifiably, at their emotional limit.

When I started my first year at this school, I can say for sure that no one thought I'd last past Christmas break. On top of trying to navigate the sometimes-heartbreaking challenges my students faced, I was only four years older than most of these kids—a fact not lost on them. If they were going to take me and our time together seriously, I had to earn their respect—no easy task. I had one thing going for me: Mark Essay. He also taught at this school, which allowed my time there to be a master class in studying under this expert teacher and learning how he captured students' attention so effectively.

Mark's approach to subtle teaching was a perfect match for my classroom of students who'd seen dozens of teachers come and go throughout their high school careers. They did not suffer fools. I was never going to win them over through rote lectures or "not smiling until Christmas." I had to use a different approach to capture their attention and try with all my might to convince them to stick with me for our ninety minutes together. So I played to my strengths—storytelling. I was able to come up with little anecdotes to open class and introduce the topic of the day in a way so subtle that they would not immediately tune me out.

This tactic was successful enough that, to my shock, I was given the Bermuda Public School's "most influential teacher" award at the end of my second year. This was a huge honor. And at the ceremony, I felt like a total fraud. That entire year, I felt in over my head and out of my depth. I had no idea what I was doing and no idea if I was making any impact on these kids.

I spent the whole year struggling to engage my students consistently. There were some days when it was obvious most students in my classroom were pretty engaged, yet I couldn't pinpoint exactly what I did that day to achieve that ever-elusive engagement. And then, of course, there were days when I lost my students early and often, and I also had no idea why. This meant that every time I sat down to plan a lesson, I was staring at a daunting blank page. I had no proven engagement formula or methodology that would make planning straightforward and optimized for engagement. So I kept trying to reinvent the wheel. Sometimes I'd get lucky, and other times my plans would fall flat. What I had going for me was a talent for getting students' attention in those first critical moments of class. After that, it really was a roll of the dice.

The truth was, as such a young and inexperienced teacher, I usually felt pretty clueless. Knowing this, my most influential teacher award revealed more about the school, the teachers, and the students than it revealed about me. Optimistically, it showed that the students really, truly wanted to be engaged in their learning. They wanted to learn and grow and were desperate for teachers to approach teaching in a way that stoked their curiosity. But there was school-wide confusion, including for me, about how to achieve this kind of teaching with consistency. This created a vacuum that left nearly all teachers in reactive mode and let a fresh-faced kid like me appear far more influential than I actually was. In the absence of a formula for engagement that instructional leaders could coach teachers to use in their classrooms, the bar for engagement was inadvertently lowered. And I was its mascot.

This is not a criticism of anyone at any school. It's what happens when educators lack productive tools that make achieving the most important aims of teaching and learning as lightweight and effective as possible. When teachers are left to reinvent the wheel of engaging teaching every day, they will inevitably burn out. They will find themselves forced to operate in reactive mode with no space or time to be proactive about much at all. But no teacher wants this! Teachers want the highest-impact strategies and tools so they can devote the majority of their time to personalizing learning, scaffolding, and nurturing healthy relationships with all students.

Winning the award made me feel like an imposter. To avoid others catching onto my fraud, I grew obsessed with dissecting the classes I designed that proved to be engaging. It became an obsession that has lasted for more than twenty years and culminated in the writing of this book. I've spent literally thousands of hours observing thousands of teachers, leaders, speakers, and even preachers to try and figure out what engaging people do differently. Ultimately, I was determined to identify engaging classes' component parts in order to back into a formula for student engagement. In doing so, designing lessons would no longer be such an intimidating and time-consuming task. And maybe, just maybe, I could eventually offer

> And inside every single one of us is an educator eager to raise the bar—to be better, more engaging, and more successful than the version of ourselves who walked into our classroom yesterday.

up an engagement formula to help myself and my fellow teachers raise the bar of our capacity to engage students. Maybe instead of only being able to reward teachers for modest wins, we could celebrate more and more of us for meeting and even exceeding higher expectations.

Maybe we could even eventually turn the tide on what has been a long pattern of educators lowering the bar in response to widespread confusion over how to engage students, or even define the concept itself. Because lowered bars only feed the feeling of being a fraud. And inside every single one of us is an educator eager to raise the bar—to be better, more engaging, and more successful than the version of ourselves who walked into our classroom yesterday.

The Engagement Predicament

Did you know that, around the 1950s, architects had a "romance with glass"?[1] This is at least according to my favorite line from a 1966 article in the Phi Delta Kappan (a K-12 research and policy journal) about the niche topic of windows and school design. Its author, Glen P. Nimnicht—an educator and researcher on the topic of early childhood education well known in the second half of the twentieth century—wrote the article in response to a shift in school design trends.[2]

Until the mid 1950s, school classrooms, apparently, had many windows. This was to let the natural light in, provide view to the outside world, and allow for critical airflow on warmer days. But in the 1950s, the cost of a portable air conditioning unit fell dramatically, such that A/C was showing up in homes, offices, and schools—to the great relief of all humans who find profuse sweating and overheating at odds with comfort and productivity.

Around the same time, educational "experts" were discussing the problem of student engagement.[3] This was not a new problem then, and it is not a new problem now. It's a problem as old as school itself. Observers were traveling from school to school and noting the lack of authentic engagement occurring in classrooms. Now you might be thinking, *What evidence were observers using to determine kids were not engaged?* You guessed it: they noticed kids were looking out all those lovely windows the architects had fallen in love with.

Every action causes an equal and opposite reaction. While comfortably cooled schools were a welcome change, school boards, facilities managers, and leaders were introduced to a new issue. The more windows there were in a classroom, the more sunlight and heat radiation that could get in, and the more costly it was to cool the classroom with air conditioning. So school architects and educational "experts" teamed up to solve the problem of economics *and* engagement.[4] Yep, they began designing classrooms with few to no windows to make temperature regulation easier and more affordable. And, to the delight of many teachers, administrators, and education experts, the removal of windows also meant the removal of the distractions of all things happening just outside their classroom windows. Voila! Lowered costs and more focused learners (insert facepalm emoji).

Or at least such an outcome was assumed. A debate followed about the humanity of learning in windowless boxes, yet no arguments prompted a change in the decades-long trend of very little natural sunlight in schools. So we stuck a bunch of fluorescent lighting panels on ceilings and justified the lack of windows by rejoicing over more wall space to hang posters that no one ever reads. Or by celebrating the ability to more easily control light to optimize media visibility. And we went on our way teaching in fluorescent boxes with minimal natural light, with all the distractions of the outside world reduced or even eliminated. Lack of student engagement, meanwhile, only grew in importance, as a matter of debate and concern and as an urgent problem in desperate search of a solution.

While Nimnicht argued in 1966 that there was a way to achieve balance between natural sunlight and *some* window exposure, that is not the point that interested me the most in his article. It was another and smaller detail that stood out to me: the relief of educators gleefully parting with the menacing distraction of…windows. This tells me three things.

One, it tells me that the obsessive-compulsive fixation on reducing costs even at the expense of students' best interests has driven far too many decisions in schools for far too long. Two, it tells me that the question of how to keep students engaged in their learning and the bad habit of looking in the wrong place for the best engagement strategies are as old as teaching itself. Three, it tells me that the tendency to imply, consciously or not, that the bar must be lowered in order for teachers to, supposedly, engage students is also nothing new, to my great dismay.

To suggest that the average teacher cannot be more engaging than a window is insulting—and flat out wrong. To suggest that teachers' capacity to engage students is wholly a function of something outside of themselves is disempowering—and flat out wrong.

Ironically, in the decades that followed Nimnicht's treatise on the romance with glass, research would go on to show the many ways fluorescent lighting was no solution. As it turns out, it can impair vision and the ability to read for many students,[5] trigger migraine headaches in students and adults,[6] reduce sleep quality at least in adults,[7] and generally crush our souls (well, I'm not sure there's research about that last point, but we know it's true). Furthermore, a 1999 study linked natural sunlight in classrooms to improved test scores.[8] Taking away that "distraction" of windows and natural light might have actually made it *harder* for teachers to engage their students.

If we want to give teachers a fighting chance at engaging students, the first thing we must do is stop making it harder for them. While you and I might lack the ability and resources to reconstruct your classroom for optimal natural light and temperature control, I hope I have the power to convince you that *you* have the power to engage your students. To the extent that engagement is a controllable process, *you* retain more control than anything or anyone—in that you and you alone have the greatest influence over how much your students engage in your classroom, windows be damned.

Why Engagement Matters

In recent years, engagement has shown up in every educator conference, every school's professional development, and every Professional Learning Network (PLN). And with good reason. Engagement has an incredible influence on student outcomes—in both directions. When students are engaged in their learning, it can yield a range of positive benefits. When they're not engaged? It can be catastrophic.

Let's start with the bad news first. Through its Gallup Student Poll, the Gallup research company routinely surveys cohorts of students to assess their views of school so that educators can understand how to create a more positive learning environment. Since its inception in 2009, the Gallup Student Poll has surveyed five million students. In their 2016 poll, taken by nearly one million U.S. students in grades 5 through 12 from 2,940 public schools and 34 private schools, Gallup identified key insights about student disengagement. Relative to their engaged classmates, disengaged students are:

- 10.0 times more likely to "strongly agree" that they do not do well in school
- 9.0 times more likely to report that they get poor grades
- 7.2 times more likely to say they feel "discouraged" about their futures
- 2.0 times more likely to report having missed a lot of school in the year prior
- More likely to state they plan to take a break after high school[9]

Gallup's research echoes other research findings about engagement. Education researchers from Johns Hopkins University and the Philadelphia Education Fund published findings of their longitudinal analyses of 13,000 students from 1994 to 2006. They were focused on how engagement in middle school impacts urban students' paths to high school graduation. Their research found a correlation between student disengagement and "detaching from school, disconnecting from its norms and expectations, reducing effort and involvement at school, and withdrawing from a commitment to school and to school completion."[10] The researchers assert that from the middle grades on, a student's repeated absenteeism, misbehavior, or low effort (and, by inference, lack of willingness to expend high effort) should be taken as clear signs that a student is actively disengaging from school and his or her path to graduation is in peril.

No surprise, then, that there's a strong link between disengagement and dropping out of school. In a 2012 American Psychological Association review of research on the student dropout problem, five core categories were found to "particularly correlate" with dropout rates: high poverty rates, poor school attendance, poor academic performance, grade retention (i.e., being held back), and, last but not least, disengagement from school.[11] Throughout school, disengagement is a red flag—and an especially alarming one from sixth grade on—that a student might be more likely to drop out. For students in high-poverty areas or for students of color, persistent disengagement should raise immediate concern, as it can practically become a predictor of dropout probability.[12]

On the other side of this dire data picture are the enormous benefits that can come when students *are* engaged in school. The same 2016 Gallup Student Poll found that, relative to their disengaged classmates, engaged students are:

- 2.5 times more likely to get "excellent" grades
- 2.5 times more likely to "strongly agree" that they perform well in school
- 4.5 times more likely to feel "hopeful" about their futures
- Far more likely to say they plan to attend a four-year college, start their own business, volunteer, or serve some sort of mission upon high school graduation[13]

The strong link between student engagement and achievement has been shown in research for decades and through a variety of lenses on engagement. In an article for NWEA (a non-profit research organization that designs assessment tools), Kathy Dyer, educator and member of the NWEA innovation team, cites research from every decade dating back to the 1960s and through the 1990s that links student engagement to improved learning outcomes.[14] As one example, classroom observations of sixth-grade students in 1968 showed that students who paid more attention in class performed better on standardized tests. In a 1972 study, researchers found a correlation between engagement in academic conversations with classmates and strong performance in school. A 1995 study asked fourth-grade teachers to rate their collective total 1,013 students' levels of engagement, which was defined as "effort and initiative taking." Researchers determined that students whose teachers ranked them high on the engagement scale also had better grades from the end of the previous year and higher scores on the Stanford Achievement Test. And in 1997, researchers analyzed the National Educational Longitudinal Study of 1988, which focused on nearly 2,000 low-income minority students in grades 8 through 12. The students who showed engagement through arriving to class on time and prepared for the day, participating in class, and making an effort to complete homework were also more academically successful and more likely to graduate high school on time than their peers who didn't demonstrate these behaviors.

While Dyer's reference to engagement research stops in the 1990s, the research on engagement did not. It continues to this day, and it continues to reveal what I believe can be taken as truth: Engagement is the antidote to students dropping out and failing to meet their potential after high school. Disengaged students are more likely to perform poorly in school, misbehave, be chronically absent, and drop out. Engaged students are more likely to perform better on tests and assignments, show up to class prepared, participate in class, interact productively with peers, graduate high school on time, and have a vision for successful plans after high school graduation. Engagement can make or break student futures.

> Engagement is the antidote to students dropping out and failing to meet their potential after high school.

The Engagement Paradox

Of the almost one million students Gallup surveyed in 2016, only 47 percent reported that they were engaged in school.[15] Twenty-nine percent

22

said they were "not engaged," and the remaining 24 percent identified themselves as "actively disengaged." Dr. Michael Schmoker—a former administrator, English teacher, and football coach turned author and education coach, whose focus is on helping educators improve student outcomes—relays research that conveys how much educators struggle to engage students. In *Results Now: How We Can Achieve Unprecedented Improvements in Teaching and Learning*, Schmoker cites a study in which researchers observed levels of student engagement in 1,500 classrooms. They found that in 85 percent of those classrooms, less than 50 percent of the students in them demonstrated engagement.[16] Put another way, more than half of students were engaged in just fifteen percent of observed classrooms. By and large, our students are checked out when in school. But data showcasing low engagement levels warrant closer inspection because they hold a paradox about engagement that every educator must know.

When averaged data of student engagement is carved up by grade level, it's revealed that as students age, they become less engaged in school. Meanwhile, in terms of students' perceived and actual future prospects, engagement grows more crucial as students age; because, as we know, the longer students remain disengaged from school, the more likely they will drop out and/or lack concrete plans after high school. Therein lies a paradox of engagement: The more students need it, the less likely they are to have it. Specifically, Gallup determined the following cascading drop in student engagement levels from fifth to twelfth grades:[17]

In fifth grade, we have a full three-fourths of our students engaged in their learning. But by the time they reach senior year, this drops to a staggering one-third. No wonder so many students at this point feel so little hope about their futures; those who have remained stuck in academic disengagement go years without the affirmation and validation that school is designed to offer them through the discovery of their skills with real-world value.

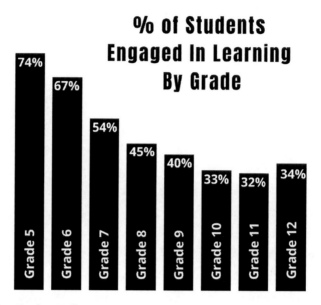

% of Students Engaged In Learning By Grade

74% — Grade 5
67% — Grade 6
54% — Grade 7
45% — Grade 8
40% — Grade 9
33% — Grade 10
32% — Grade 11
34% — Grade 12

Data: Gallup Student Poll, 2016

Many people have attempted to identify why engagement drops as students age. Ask ten people, and you'll get ten different opinions. Some might say it's because school gets more challenging and, as a result, harder to remain engaged in as grades advance. Others blame the obsession on standardized test scores over the deep learning that matters to students' futures. Someone else will point out that so long as a school remains stuck in the industrial model, students will see it as irrelevant to the dynamic digital worlds in which they live. Others blame a dearth of alternative pathways for those who don't want to attend four-year college. Some will make the point that puberty itself is a distraction, and social and relationship challenges tend to multiply and preoccupy kids as they get older. Finally, many cite the advent of smartphones and social media, which they argue have done serious damage to students' capacity to sustain focus in school and their learning.

While identifying the root cause of students' declining engagement has value, fixating on it for too long will miss the point. And the point is that we must figure out how to empower ALL teachers to engage ALL students every day and throughout the day. When it comes to the engagement data, no one is off the hook of implementing an intentional daily engagement plan. While elementary students are, statistically, more likely to be engaged in their learning, this data is just that—a statistic. Our students are humans, and we have to be honest about how many of them might be engaged in our personal elementary classrooms. And we have to strive for one hundred percent of our students to be engaged. Because given what we know about the trajectory of engagement as students age, elementary school teachers have the power to get kids so engaged in their learning today that they are insulated against engagement decline in later grades. The kind of engagement that prevents dropping out of high school doesn't start in high school; it starts in elementary school. As for secondary teachers, while your students have more of the natural distractions of hormonal changes and increasingly complex social lives, these cannot become excuses to take our eye off the engagement ball for even one student.

Why Engagement Remains Elusive

In 2018, Gallup asked nearly 2,000 public school superintendents to rank order seven factors for measuring the effectiveness of public schools in their communities. Their top concern? Student engagement. Ninety-one percent of these superintendents deemed engagement vital to assessing the success of their schools.[18] Only nine percent ranked standardized test scores, which came in last on the list. By the way, in 2016 Gallup found in the same survey that 83 percent of public school superintendents ranked student engagement as the most important factor of success.[19]

Given what we know about engagement's power to keep kids in class, on time, prepared, and ready to grow, learn, and meet their potential, the value superintendents place on engagement makes sense. The fact that engagement is a near-daily topic of conversation in schools and a frequent focus of professional learning also makes sense. Yet its prevalence as a focus of instruction and a classroom goal hasn't given way to meaningfully increased levels of student engagement and improved outcomes—to the great frustration of countless well-meaning educators. Nor has the flood of engagement "experts" promising some magic bullet. What gives?

I've been fortunate enough to travel across the United States and internationally to support educators in exceeding their potential and helping their students do the same. Working alongside so many educators in the field affords more benefits than I can count. Most significantly, it gives me the profound gratification of meeting and knowing thousands of incredible educators and witnessing firsthand just how much teachers across the country and around the globe care about children and want to do right by their students. It also allows me to see a strange and pervasive phenomenon in education: The more pressure we put on teachers to do "X" thing successfully and effectively or implement the latest must-have instructional technique or tool, the more we take them—the experts of their classrooms and their students—out of the equation. The more critical a priority becomes, the more heavy-handed the approach becomes and the less we enable teacher agency in deciding how to achieve the thing in question.

We saw this when it came to blended learning. The pressure to get technologies into schools came on fast and furious—and justifiably so. If schools cannot teach students career-ready technology skills and digital savvy, schools will fundamentally lack relevance. But optics, not pedagogy, drove rapid decisions in the early days of school tech adoption. This led to haphazard, draconian professional development that all too often removed teachers—and all their wisdom, agency, and creativity—from making learning-focused technology decisions with *their* students in mind. Ultimately, after the limits—both on teaching and learning—of this approach made themselves known, we had to reorient blended learning around empowering teachers to use technology to enhance their instructional efficacy and learning outcomes.

In fact, we see this pattern almost every time a concept becomes a must-have in education. We saw this happen with learning relationships and social-emotional wellness. Both matter deeply when it comes to improving student outcomes and bringing greater relevance and a future focus to learning. In the early days of their respective adoptions, optics once again drove the car. Speed was prioritized over pedagogy, and teachers were relegated to being didactically taught how to relate to their students rather than empowered with best practices that they were then free to adapt to the individuals in their classrooms.

Putting Engagement Back in Your Hands

When it comes to learning, students are the most important part of the equation. But when it comes to instruction, teachers are the most important of the equation. When they are taken out of it, we see it and we feel it. Learning outcomes fall. Teacher frustration and stress skyrocket. Pressure on administrators to improve test scores grows that much more intense. And students become less and less engaged in their education. Once engagement is lost, the task to restore it becomes that much more Herculean, triggering a vicious cycle of yet more stress on teachers and more pressure on administrators to improve increasingly-out-of reach student performance through heavy-handed measures that further disempower teachers. Whew!

As I set out to achieve with blended learning in my first book,

> When it comes to learning, students are the most important part of the equation. But when it comes to instruction, teachers are the most important of the equation.

Bold School: Old School Wisdom + New School Technologies = Blended Learning That Works, and—alongside my wife and co-author, Molly— with learning relationships in *Breaking Bold: Dare to Defy the Tyranny of Trends and Live the Relationship Habits of a Master Educator*, I am seeking with this book to restore teachers to their rightful place in the engagement equation. When it comes to engaging students in their learning, confusion abounds. In my opinion, this is because the prevailing engagement tools and strategies taught to teachers have curtailed their agency. Instead of giving teachers a general formula or roadmap, we've pushed engagement strategies and tools on them that are overly prescriptive. Such that, when teachers try to apply them, they find them too confining, without enough room for them to play to their strengths, or a misfit for their particular students. So the tools and strategies prove their inherently short lifespans once again and fail—to the great frustration of thousands of sincere, hardworking teachers out there and at steep costs to students. And all this, only if teachers are even offered engagement strategies at all.

As I reverse-engineered those of my classes that ended up achieving high levels of student engagement and began to do the same with other master teachers, I began to notice a pattern. I put titles to each of the component parts of engaging classes, as well as engaging workshops, lectures, and sermons. I began to distill engagement to its very essence. To map it. To define each of its elements. Lo and behold, I found it was working. With more consistency, and for reasons I could now explain, I was planning for engaging learning. Over the years, I tested and refined this engagement formula more and more. I began sharing it with colleagues, and their feedback helped me improve upon it.

By the time I started coaching teachers, I had a heavily-vetted engagement formula with a track record of success. Importantly and by design, it kept teachers at the center of decisions and students at the center of learning. It gave teachers room to leverage their strengths and tailor learning to students while also minimizing risks of disengagement. The formula offered a plan to engage students in deep learning. It was both reliably consistent and flexible, both guiding and empowering. And, unlike so many approaches to engagement, it does not condescend to teachers, and it does not lower the bar. This formula believes in you, and it cannot work without all the skill and wisdom you bring to it.

Engagement is far too important to burden teachers with authoritative, rigid, vague, or complicated strategies that leave no space for them. Engagement is far too important to merely cross our fingers and hope teachers figure it out on their own. If history tells us anything, some will figure it out on their own, many won't, and others will try so hard to chase it that they'll run themselves right out of the profession.

> Engagement is far too important to merely cross our fingers and hope teachers figure it out on their own. If history tells us anything, some will figure it out on their own, many won't, and others will try so hard to chase it that they'll run themselves right out of the profession.

With this book, my aim is to put you back in the driver's seat of engaging *your* students. Not only do I hope to provide you with a roadmap that keeps your decision-making ability firmly intact, but I also hope to provide you with a roadmap that allows you to get creative and have some fun along the way. Because, as it turns out, it is through your creativity—not some constricting, so-called magic bullet—that your students will want to engage in their learning, from remaining curious about it, to participating wholeheartedly in the work, and to persevering through the typical highs and lows of growth in order to reap the rewards of engagement.

You have all you need to boldly engage students. It's easier than it may look, and the formula has been right in front of you all along.

CHAPTER 2

The Engagement Formula

A few years ago, when I was coaching educators at a middle school, I took my seat in the back of a sixth-grade math class. The teacher settled into her place at the front of a classroom and then, in a move I'd not seen before, held a banana high in her hand. As her students began to file into the room and sit in their seats, naturally they were curious as to why their teacher was holding a single banana next to her head.

"Miss Curry, why are you holding a banana?" a student asked. She didn't answer. Then another student came in and asked the same question. No answer. She stood upfront in mysterious silence, just holding that banana—already a risky move in front of middle school students.

Finally, once all the students were seated, Miss Curry broke her silence. "How fast do you all think you could eat this entire banana?"

Immediately, the room erupted. Kids were throwing out times. They were challenging each other's guess. And because every kid needs to be heard, a handful of them declared they don't even like bananas anyway. Miss Curry allowed the kids to discuss for a minute or two.

Meanwhile, I sat confused and quiet, in the back of the classroom. Where on earth is she going with this?

"OK," Miss Curry said. "Let me ask you a different question. Raise your hand if you think you could eat this entire banana in less than one minute and keep 'em raised."

Most of the students in the classroom raised their hands in affirmation.

"How about forty-five seconds?" she asked. A few hands dropped. "Thirty seconds?" Several students put their hands down. She continued lowering the number of seconds, and more and more hands continued to drop. Until she arrived, to nobody's surprise, at two boys jockeying it out for potassium-fueled greatness.

James, the most enthusiastic of the two, shouted, "I can eat that banana in seven seconds!"

Miss Curry responded in disbelief, "James, you think you can eat this entire banana in seven seconds?"

"Yes!" James answered. "I think I can eat it in *seven* seconds." Gauntlet—thrown.

At that moment, I could feel every kid in that classroom think the exact same thought: *Please, for the love…Let James try to eat this banana in front of us in seven seconds.*

"OK, James, so you think you can eat this entire banana in seven seconds. Come up to the front of the room and take my chair. I'm going to get out my phone to time you." Miss Curry handed the banana to James and grabbed her phone. All eyes were on him—could he really do it? Could he actually eat that banana in seven seconds? Or were we all about to witness a colossal disaster that may or may not end in puking? Either way, the kids and I were dialed in. Miss Curry cued him to prepare: "OK, class, James says he can eat this entire banana in seven seconds. James, on your mark…get set…go!"

Furiously, James began peeling the banana.

"Whoa whoa whoa!" Miss Curry interjected. "What are you doing?"

James's face was contorted in confusion. "I'm peeling the banana. So I can eat it in seven seconds," he said.

"But that's not my challenge," Miss Curry said.

"It's not?" James asked quizzically.

"No," Miss Curry said. "I asked you how fast you could eat the *entire* banana."

James's eyes widened to saucers as he and his classmates were hit with the same realization you're having right now. Instantly, everyone understood the verbal trick Miss Curry had played on them and what it meant for poor James, who committed to eating an *entire* banana in seven seconds!

James desperately tried to negotiate. "Come on Miss Curry! I have to peel it, and *then* I can eat this banana in seven seconds!"

"So you're telling me that if you peel the banana first and then eat it, you can eat the banana in seven seconds?"

"Yeah, that's what I meant. That's what I thought you meant," James said in defeat.

"So, James, do you think the order in which you do this matters?"

"Yes," James said. "It does!"

"That's right!" She turned to the class and, with enthusiasm, said, "So we can all agree—*order matters.*"

And so began Mrs. Curry's lesson on order of operations. In a word: incredible. It was a remarkable start to a topic that can, at face value, appear uninteresting. But in Miss Curry's hands, it was anything but.

Contrast how she started that class with another option: "Good morning, class. Today we're going to talk about order of operations." Snooze. Frankly, most kids would probably rather choke on a banana. James sure would have. That would be like me kicking off this book by saying, "Good day, readers. Today we're going to talk about student engagement." I would have lost you before we even started.

Just as you were when you picked up this book, students are curious. They walk into our classrooms every day filled with curiosity. It's true.

Think about it—they give us the evidence. Because, every day, they ask us the same ridiculous question: "What are we doing today?" Or my favorite from high school students: "Are we doing anything today?" As perplexing as these questions may feel to us teachers—who painstakingly plan some form of "doing" for students every day—what they are telling us is that they don't want to be bored. They *want* to be engaged. Any human who's been around a three-year-old knows that we come into this life naturally hungry to grapple with ideas and concepts. We are willing to struggle and sort through new information to achieve learning. The extent to which we, as educators, can ignite and hold students' curiosity—such that they'll participate in their learning and stick with it when it gets hard—is a function of if and how we engage them, from the first moments of class to the last.

> The extent to which we, as educators, can ignite and hold students' curiosity—such that they'll participate in their learning and stick with it when it gets hard—is a function of if and how we engage them, from the first moments of class to the last.

The Creativity Formula

When I witnessed Miss Curry's bananas banana introduction (had to, it'll be the only time, promise) to order of operations, I was taken by how creative it was. Yet it was so simple and effective in grabbing her kids' attention in the first minutes of class and convincing them that the learning which would follow was important and worth engaging in and persisting through. It was such a perfect example of applying a dose of creativity to engage students that I've shared it with scores of educators in an attempt to showcase how straightforward it can be to stoke your students' curiosity early and often. The first few times I relayed this story to my colleagues in education, I noticed something. Most every teacher was impressed with Miss Curry's clever tactic to engage students from the start of class. But their admiration was almost always followed with a justification for why nothing like it would show up in their own classrooms. "I would never think of anything like that," some would say. Or "I'm just not that creative."

This dismayed and discouraged me. I shared the banana story to show how easy and wonderful it can be to spark curiosity and set yourself and your students up for engagement, not to deflate anyone's confidence or make them feel inadequate! What Miss Curry did was so simple—she thought of an everyday activity (eating a banana) that any child could relate to and where the order in which it's approached matters. In this, she found a hook to introduce order of operations and prime her students for engaging learning. If the average adult reflexively responded to this little creative act of engagement with self-doubt, then I knew we needed to have a conversation about creativity. I believe in teachers, and I believe *every* teacher—every last one of you!—has the capacity to be creative, every day. If you've shown up here, then you have the curiosity and the drive to learn how to unlock the creative genius in you. Learning to discover and channel that creative genius is the most important part of learning to engage students in your classroom. Because creativity is the backdrop to creating engaging learning experiences.

We love creativity in our culture. So much so that we put it on the highest of pedestals. Creativity is the lifeblood of innovation and progress. It matters and deserves respect. But I am here to knock it down to size. While creativity is admirable and significant, it's not nearly as inaccessible as we've been led to believe. So let's put creativity in its rightful place—on your standard issue counter stool. A high quality and sturdy one, yes! But one that any average adult or tall child can reach with no problem.

The dictionary definition of *creativity* is "the ability to create" and "the quality of being creative."[1] Boom. That's it. Note that this definition does not include "the ability to create something entirely novel, innovative, heretofore unseen or unknown to humankind." Or "the quality of being like Steve Jobs, Frida Kahlo, Louis Armstrong, Marie Curie, Albert Einstein, or other such rarefied inventors and creators, those few super-humans who are able to think up and act on ideas, concepts, or hypotheses that us mere mortals are incapable of doing and therefore leave us feeling like plain dolts, disappointments, and imposters throughout life." Nope. To be creative is to create. Period.

What you create can be as small but powerful as an interesting hook to a lesson that pulls your students in and excites them to learn. Or it can be the next iPhone, whatever that may be. (And you know what, if you know that, while my M.O. is to promote teacher empowerment and retention, maybe you should put this book down and go make your billions.) In terms of how you relate to creativity, my desire for you is the same as my desire for our children—I'm less interested in *what* you create than making sure you believe you *can* create. When it comes to engagement, it begins by finding a relatable "in" that will ignite your kids' curiosity at the start of class and follows with a plan mapped out in advance to sustain that curiosity, and the enthusiasm that comes with it, throughout.

The news about creativity gets better even from there. The world's most creative and engaging educators don't create in a vacuum or start from square one—and nor should you. As they do, you also can—and should—rely on the shoulders of all those who've created before you. In fact, this is the best path to unleashing the kind of creativity you need in order to engage students. Because...drumroll please: *Creativity is formulaic*. And I'll prove it.

Nothing is invented out of nowhere. Nothing. The iPhone as we know it today was inspired by the Blackberry (which was an evolution upon the mobile phone) and evolved from the iPod (which was a

Walkman on steroids). And, by the way, Steve Jobs had to be talked into the idea of Apple building a phone—an idea he staunchly opposed for many years. Even the supernaturally creative have ruts or get it wrong sometimes.[2] Einstein's theory of relativity was made possible only by the creative thinking and experimentation of Galileo Galilei (he looked up at the stars one night and decided to ponder them), Isaac Newton (who watched an apple fall from a tree and wondered why), and other scientists who paved the way. Frida Kahlo drew influence from European Renaissance masters, Mexican post-revolutionary romanticism and nationalism, and her infamous and painful bus accident, among other artists and personal events. Creativity is about knowing where to look for inspiration. It is not something one has or doesn't have, and it's not something that only a select few have. It is, in fact, abundant and exists in all of us.

Countless people you (rightly) perceive as talented creatives draw inspiration from formulas, as crafted and honed by those who came before them and proved their viability. To showcase this creative reality, we're going to play a little game.

Quick: What do Aretha Franklin's "Respect," Judy Garland's "Over the Rainbow," Prince's "When Doves Cry," and Nirvana's "Smells Like Teen Spirit" have in common? You might say, *Not much!* As it turns out, they have a lot in common. Most significantly, they were all created upon the same framework.

In 2015, Mick Grierson—a computer scientist, musician, and professor at Goldsmiths, University of London—was curious as to what makes a hit song, well, a hit. To determine this, he needed to

> Creativity is about knowing where to look for inspiration. It is not something one has or doesn't have, and it's not something that only a select few have. It is, in fact, abundant and exists in all of us.

produce a list of the fifty most iconic pop songs ever composed. He compiled a meta-list from hundreds of "all-time best" lists from popular music magazines, such as *Rolling Stone* and *NME*, as well as lists from major newspapers across decades to arrive at the fifty songs that appeared most often on all lists.[3] Computer scientist that he is, he then plugged the songs into analytical software to look for patterns, if any, that existed across all or most of the songs. All told, Grierson discovered that nearly all the songs followed a similar pattern: Eighty percent of the songs were in a major key, and a similar share were in the A, E, C, or G keys. The average song tempo was 125 beats per minute, with 40 percent being slightly slower at 120 beats per minute. Nearly all had 500 beats, and the songs had between six and eight chord changes. Even without Grierson's analysis, we all know that most every song follows the verse 1-chorus-verse 2-chorus-bridge-verse 3-chorus flow.

What about movies? Let's take some blockbusters, like *Star Wars*, *Harry Potter*, *The Matrix*, *Spider-Man*, and *The Lord of the Rings*. The specifics of these movies run the gamut—from Jabba the Hutt to a lightning bolt-marked child magician to the red pill vs. blue pill, showing that uniqueness is alive and well among these films. Yet each follows the iconic hero's journey formula. In this story structure, a protagonist sets out on some sort of journey in unknown territory, meets people (or fantastical beings) integral to their path, encounters a roadblock or challenge, confronts a nemesis, and eventually returns home a changed person.

Ever heard of Freytag's pyramid? Probably not. Ever seen a Disney movie? Obviously. Nearly every Disney movie you've ever seen and loved follows Freytag's Pyramid, which was identified by novelist Gustav Freytag in the nineteenth century. At that point, the structure was already as old as time and had been captured in stories and myths for millennia. Freytag simply noticed the pattern and put terminology to it. It starts with "exposition," where the story elements and characters are introduced and explained. The "rising action" comes next, which is where a conflict is introduced and escalates. Eventually, this drama reaches a "climax," where all the tension comes to a head. Then there is a "falling action," where the aftermath of the climax is explored. Finally, there is "resolution," where loose ends are tied, and the story is brought to some sort of close.

Think about *The Lion King*. In the opening scene, King Mufasa delivers us **exposition**. "Everything the light touches will be yours one day," Mufasa explains to his son, Simba. After some scenes showing Mufasa training Simba for the throne, we are then taken to the **inciting incident** (spoiler alert): Simba is lured into a stampede and Mufasa is subsequently killed in the chaos. Simba, who sees himself as having played a role in his father's death, is racked with guilt and leaves Pride Rock. Fortunately, he meets Timon and Pumbaa (a meerkat and warthog, respectively), who help him heal, mature, grow, and move on. That's our **rising action**. But we all know hakuna matata can't last forever. This leads us to the **climax**, Simba's final face off with Scar. After a ferocious fight, we segue into the **falling action**—a literary device that is no mere device for Disney. Oh no, they love to go literal with this one—Mother Gothel in *Tangled*, Gaston in *Beauty and the Beast*, Syndrome in the *Incredibles*—notice anything similar about their demise? Yep, actual falling! Scar is no different. Eventually, Scar falls into a pit with a menacing pack of hyenas and, well, lights out for Scar. In the **resolution**, the newly confident Simba takes his place as the King of Pride Rock. And the circle of life continues. There you have it—Freytag's Pyramid, Disney style. (Note: My wife just pointed out that I have a *Lion King* reference in *Bold School*. So I love *The Lion King*! I'm not ashamed to show my soft side.)

While the foundational formulas of creativity are too many to include here, I'll share just one more with you. On a recent flight, I was looking forward to the opportunity for unbroken alone time to get some work done. To my great dismay, it appeared that the Wi-Fi wasn't working. So I hit my call button. You know the world is stressed when even a Southwest attendant is short-tempered.

When the attendant approached me, I politely asked, "Is the internet down?"

"Yeah," she said. "Pretend like it's the olden days," and then walked off.

Pretend like it's the olden days!? I thought. This, from the airline with a heart in its name? Well, if that heart means nothing to you, it means nothing to me either. You want me to pretend like it's the olden days, then I'll pretend like it's the olden days, alright.

So...I lit up a cigarette.

The flight attendant hustled back to me in a huff. "What do you think you're doing? You can't smoke on a plane, it's illegal!"

"Well then, pretend like it isn't." I said.

In case any of you double as flight marshals, one, that's awesome. Two, this is NOT a true story. I don't want you to think Kieschnick is out there lighting up cigarettes on airplanes. So why did I share this fake story? To make the point that almost every joke or funny story you've ever heard follows an almost identical formula. My story is no different.

The formula goes like this: It starts with the "setup," which in this case was all the detail up to the point of the flight attendant's sarcastic remark. Then there's an "assumption," where the listener is led to assume that the story will unfold in a certain direction. In the case of my joke, that assumption might have been that I did as I was told and started shopping in SkyMall for a Bigfoot the Garden Yeti statue or Smittens, the mittens that let you hold your own hands within mittens. But then a joke "shatters the assumption," which was me lighting a cigarette. Lastly is the "punchline," where I told the flight attendant to pretend smoking on a plane was not illegal. The number of clever and unique jokes (I'm not claiming mine is!) that have followed this universal formula is infinite.

Therein lies a critical point: These formulas are just that—formulas. They include structure, guidelines, parameters. Professors from Columbia Business School and INSEAD teamed up to see if they could determine why popular culture becomes popular. They analyzed 60 years' worth of songs from the Billboard Hot 100 across eight song characteristics, like "danceability," "instrumentalness," and "acousticness." They determined that the songs that charted the highest "simultaneously conform to prevailing musical feature profiles while exhibiting some degree of individuality or novelty."[4] They go on to say, "They sound similar to whatever else is popular at the time, but also have enough of a unique sound to help them stand out as distinctive." The upshot? These hit songs are the same but different, as the saying goes. They followed what was fashionable at the time but with a unique spin on it. They were not novel to the world or created out of thin air.

Creativity is where formula meets imagination. The formulas are not recipes, where every ingredient, and in what precise order and measure, is explicitly laid out. They themselves are like a great teacher—they guide creativity without prescribing it. They leave room for the person applying a formula to bring their own ideas, knowledge, experiences, wisdom, and self to the ultimate

> Creativity is where formula meets imagination.

creation. But knowing a dependable creativity formula is the heaviest lift in the work of creating something people will respond to positively.

If you're unaware that the world is chock full of formulas for various creative endeavors, it's easy to see how creativity can appear uncanny and out of reach. It is true that the cleverness built upon formulas is as unique to the person doing the creating, such that it can seem original. But hopefully you see now just how much creativity is formulaic. And achieving it is simply bringing your greatest asset—*you*—to a preexisting formula.

Creating engagement in our classrooms is no different. Once you have the formula, you can create a specific plan to excite and engage your students—as many as humanly possible, throughout a lesson, and every day. And perhaps most importantly—you, not someone or something else, will be in control of the approach to engaging your students. The bar need not be lowered to the point of removing all the windows in your classroom because distractions are no match for your creative prowess.

Engagement Defined: A Three-Point Concept to Eradicate Confusion—*Finally*

Before we dive into the engagement formula, we must define engagement. Part of the confusion around engagement is that there are a million definitions of it out there, some stronger than others. In this blizzard of definitions, it's no wonder educators feel so confused as to what engagement is, much less how to elicit it from their students.

With so many conflicting and often vague definitions of student engagement in the world, many educators simply throw up their arms and equate student engagement to fun. I don't blame teachers for this, as students having fun can certainly, at least at face value, look like engagement. But let me be clear: By engagement, I do not mean fun. I'm not trying to turn you into the "fun" teacher. Whether as former students ourselves, educators, or parents, we all know what the "fun" classroom looks like. It's the classroom with marshmallows and cooked spaghetti strewn about that kids mess around with in the name of some sort of experiment. When you ask the kids in that classroom what they did at school today, they say, "We played with spaghetti and ate marshmallows!" They rarely remark on what they learned.

Authentic engagement results in learning so fascinating, relevant, challenging, and exciting that it compels students to enthusiastically share it with others and ultimately put their newly acquired knowledge to use. It's not enough to engage students in fun—we are not in the business of "edutainment." Instead, we must engage them in the deep learning that will unlock all those benefits we reviewed in Chapter 1—the benefits that keep students engaged as they age, all the way through to graduation, with a clear, post-high school plan and a strong belief in their potential.

In a 2016 paper, "The Meanings of Student Engagement: Implications for Policies and Practices," educational researchers Paul Ashwin and Debbie McVitty explore the confusion around engagement's meaning and various definitions.[5] One of their points is to show that this confusion makes it extremely difficult to decide which actions to take in order to achieve engagement. They cite a series of reasons as to why so many definitions differ, conflict, and seem vague to the point of impossibility in grasping how to work with a given definition. They argue that the *object* or focus of student engagement—what it is students are engaging with—can vary, both across definitions and as students age, leading to confusion. Objects can include learning activities, a subject-area course at large, or a knowledge set. They point out that the *formation* of engagement can also vary. Engaged students can be "forming" individual understanding. They can form curricula, meaning their engagement can shape and influence the what, why, and how of their learning. Or they can form communities, meaning they can be engaged in shaping the institutions and societies in which they are involved (Ashwin and McVitty point out that this form or engagement is more relevant at the level of higher education).

Ashwin and McVitty raise important points about how difficult it is to land upon one definition of engagement, particularly one that is elucidating to educators as to how to achieve it. But therein lies the rub: Nearly every definition of engagement excludes educators. Nearly every definition of engagement only speaks to students. Nearly every definition stops short of giving insight into how educators can achieve the things that, per this approach to defining engagement, students are doing or demonstrating when engaged in school.

Education researcher I am not. Educator and coach, however, I am. As I said in Chapter 1, so many of the problems we face in education come when we take educators out of the equation. Every time we dis-empower teachers, we create a problem. Usually, this disempowerment happens as we attempt to solve an original problem. So we layer a prob-lem with a new problem...and think this will solve problems?

My promise to you is that we will not do that here. We will not take away your agency when it comes to engagement, such that we make the problem of engagement more problematic. Nor will we subscribe to some sort of pie-in-the-sky notion that it is possible to engage all your students, in every minute of class, every day. It's not. And we'll talk about why later. Instead, I'm going to provide a definition of engage-ment that, once and for all, places *you* as an active player in it.

I propose a three-point definition of engagement, one that includes all the key players and realities so that it can be an actionable con-cept. As a summarizing and memory tool, engagement can be dis-tilled down to an *observation of*, a *function of*, and *achievement of* three essential parts.

Let me explain. Our definition of engagement is premised on what is observable in engaged students (or absent in disengaged students). But we will not stop there. To stop there would be to keep educators stuck and powerless in a vague and inactionable definition of engage-ment. So from there, our definition will showcase what teachers can and cannot influence when it comes to student engagement; that is, define what engagement is a function of so teachers can focus on the aspects of the equation they can control. Lastly, it will give educators the action roadmap to engagement so teachers can leverage what's in their power to achieve engagement to the point of its observability in students.

Most importantly, our three-point definition will prepare you to yield all those delicious fruits of engagement's labor. After all, we know that the outcome of student engagement is not "fun." It's showing up to class every day, on time, ready to learn. It's stronger classroom relation-ships, improved grades and test scores, the opening up of how students perceive their skills and their futures. And it's feeding a belief so strong in their potential that they begin to formulate post-high school plans—and then set out to achieve them.

Engagement Defined: Part 1—Engagement as Observed in Students

The first part of defining engagement is defining what it means as it pertains to students; that is, what it looks like when students are engaged in their learning. Having pored over research-based definitions of engagement and synthesized the strongest ones into a simple and memorable concept, I propose the following definition of engagement, part 1: Student engagement is *curiosity, participation, and perseverance.*

Engagement Defined: Part 1—Engagement as Observed in Students:
Curiosity
Participation
Perseverance

More specifically, engagement happens when student curiosity is stoked, students are actively participating in their learning, and they feel the desire to persevere no matter the challenge before them, the perceived difficulty of the task, or roadblocks they confront.

In this definition of engagement's first part, we are reminded that engagement itself is not the main event. The main event is learning. But without this definition of engagement, learning doesn't stand a chance. Because if curiosity is squashed, then students will be depleted of the motivation to participate in their learning, and it won't occur to them to persevere through struggle. Curiosity, participation, and perseverance are the channels through which kids will be motivated to engage in their learning. When repeatedly engaged over time, students will achieve all the vital benefits of engagement.

Engagement Defined: Part 2—Engagement as a Function of What You Can Control

Making explicit what student engagement is a function of is a *must*. Because in doing so, we are reminded of an indisputable truth upon which successfully achieving engagement is contingent: You have only so much control over your students, and it's really not much. To engage them, focus on what you can control. Any definition that leaves room for teachers to try to control the uncontrollable falls short and might cause teachers to spin their wheels to the point of madness.

Engagement Defined: Part 2—Engagement as a Function of Student Disposition and Teaching Methodology

$$E = f(SD + TM)$$

E = engagement, SD = student disposition,
TM = teaching methodology

We cannot control our students' dispositions. That is part their nature, part what is going on with them on a given day, and part of their larger life circumstances. We can, however, control our teaching methodology. We can control the instructional strategies we choose to use. We can decide what is the best application of technology tools so they enhance learning and your effectiveness. We can choose the learning task we ask students to complete. And we absolutely have the power to approach a lesson with the express goal of engaging and re-engaging our students throughout. That brings us to Part 3 of our definition of engagement.

Engagement Defined: Part 3—Engagement as Achieved by Teachers

This is the part of the definition that I am most concerned with and excited about. Because it's here that we finally clear up so much

46

confusion about how to achieve those observable elements of engaged students. It's here that we can focus on the ways we can reach students to engage them in their learning, rather than trying to influence things over which we have no influence. It's here that teachers can unleash their creativity in order to stoke students' curiosity, convince them that the learning is fascinating enough to participate in, and inspire them to persevere through challenges.

And it's here where we can finally have a definition of engagement that includes you, the teacher. Because this is where we can leverage a formula for student engagement that can function as a holistic teaching methodology. It's through a formula that you can think of a bananas banana introduction (OK, last time, I swear!) like Miss Curry's to your class and follow it with a roadmap designed to keep students engaged and re-engaged throughout, even when it naturally drops, thanks to their dispositions.

It's here where *ATLAS* lives.

ATLAS: The Formula for Engagement That Leaves You in the Driver's Seat

ATLAS is our creative engagement formula and the purpose of this book. It is an acronym for a teaching methodology you can plug into the engagement equation in order to complete it. It is the crux of the third and final part of our definition of engagement.

Engagement Defined: Part 3—Engagement as Achieved by Teachers

Attention: The intentional opener to class that stokes students' curiosity and compels them to participate in the learning to follow

Transition: The schematic bridge between something familiar in the Attention getter and the new content to come

Lesson: The transference of hierarchically-presented priority points that support students' retention of the information

Activity: The metacognitive action students take with new information to reinforce retention and catalyze deep learning and understanding

Summation: The intentional connection of priority points to positive emotion to boost student self-efficacy

ATLAS is a formula built upon research, thousands of classroom observations, and time-tested experience that will leave you—the only expert I care about, and the one who happens to know your students best—firmly at its center. With you in creative control of this formula, you are free to layer it with all your agency, wisdom, knowledge, and insights about your students. You are empowered to devote your time and effort only to what you can control as you elicit the observable indicators of student engagement. And you are empowered to help your students achieve the fruits of engagement.

Refresh: Engagement Defined

*Our three-point definition of engagement that puts
teachers back in the driver's seat*

Part 1—Engagement as Observed in Students
Curiosity
Participation
Perseverance

*Part 2—Engagement as a Function of Student
Disposition and Teaching Methodology*
E = f(SD + TM)
E = engagement, SD = student disposition, TM = teaching
methodology

Part 3—Engagement as Achieved by Teachers
Attention
Transition
Lesson
Activity
Summation

The Power of *ATLAS*

The beauty of our three-part definition of engagement is that it builds the *how* into engagement with just the right mix of structure and flexibility. In following *ATLAS*, not only does deeper learning stand a chance, but it is also set up to be a guarantee. Along the way, I expect you will discover your creative genius, learn how to channel it, and see how satisfying and fun it is to inject it into your own practice—to the priceless effect of creating that magical alchemy of kids deeply engrossed and engaged in what they're learning–about a concept *and* themselves.

ATLAS also has a built-in answer to the reality of dealing with humans, especially those of the child variety. You will not keep any student engaged for every minute of every class no matter what you do. Anyone who tells you it's possible is

> At best, engagement looks like the letter "W," with peaks and valleys.

a fool, and you can tell them I said it. At best, engagement looks like the letter "W," with peaks and valleys. *ATLAS* ensures that you will capture student attention in the first moments of class. But it will inevitably dip, and you'll have to re-engage students. Then their attention will dip again, and you'll have to re-engage them again. Maybe, and especially in longer classes, you might lose your students again and have to re-engage them. The "W" nature of engagement is simply a fact of human nature, not a fault or failing on your part.

ENGAGEMENT

The great news about *ATLAS* is that, while in the *ATLAS* order we get a handy acronym, you do not have to remain faithful to the order. While all classes are best served when opened with attention and closed with summation, you can use all five components in any order that optimizes student engagement throughout the class. Think of *ATLAS* as a sandbox. A sandbox has borders and boundaries, but what happens inside of it is infinite. The *ATLAS* model is similar.

In the following five chapters, we'll take a closer look at each of its five components, including how they relate to each other. It will become apparent that, in the first use of *ATLAS* in a given class session, you will likely follow the A-T-L-A-S flow. But when it comes time to re-engage students, you can lean on any of the five components and in any order. You might find it productive to return to a new attention getter to reignite your students' curiosity. Perhaps you'll need to transfer additional new information to students. Maybe you'll want to include a second activity for more challenging content delivered in the lesson. Or maybe you'll need to connect a point to positive or inspiring emotion to summarize the relevance and meaning of the learning and give students a little confidence boost.

The point is that *ATLAS* puts the power in your hands—always within a malleable structure. You won't have to come up with some re-engagement strategy out of thin air. Instead, you can pre-plan it by drawing from the *ATLAS* components most appropriate to your lesson and your students.

First, let's hop into the driver's seat and take a closer look at each of *ATLAS*'s five components. Let's help cultivate the creative genius that already lives within you, with roadmap in hand to become prepared and empowered masters of engagement.

CHAPTER 3

Attention

Please tell me you've watched *Ted Lasso*. This show is many things. It's a comedy about a fun-loving, Midwestern football coach from the University of Kansas who is recruited to coach football—the American soccer kind—in London. Yet the show manages to be funny without an ounce of cynicism. Instead, vulnerability—the Brené Brown, emotional kind—heart, compassion, forgiveness, honesty, and leading with kindness are the backdrop to comedic moments.

Coach Ted Lasso, played by SNL alum Jason Sudeikis, has a knack for witticisms, memorable sayings, and great one-liners. One such example is when, in the first season, one of his players, Sam, is frustrated after having a bad practice.

Coach Lasso pulls Sam over to the sidelines of the field and asks him, "You know what the happiest animal on earth is?" Sam stares at him blankly. "It's a goldfish," Coach Lasso says. "You know why?"

Sam answers no and shakes his head in confusion.

"Got a ten-second memory." Coach Lasso smiles and says, "Be a goldfish, Sam."

For all the show's integrity, as it turns out Coach Lasso has this one wrong. Goldfish do not have a ten-second memory. Nor do they have attention spans so short that nothing can be transferred to their memories—as is commonly believed. This isn't the first time these little fish have been slandered either! Their unfair bad rap can be traced back to a 2015 report about (human) attention span published by Microsoft.[1] In the report, its authors wrote that the average person's attention span had dropped from 12 seconds to 8 seconds in just a decade. For shock value, the authors pointed out that with human attention span lasting a mere eight seconds, even goldfish have superior attention spans.

For those of you out there passionate about defending the goldfish's good name (all nine of you), I'm happy to report that the idea that they have teeny attention spans and memories is pure myth. In fact, fish researchers have conducted experiments that reveal goldfish have attention capacity and memories so robust they can remember events they experienced only one time a full year later.[2] So impressive are their miniature brains that goldfish are often used as the common model to study cognition in other fish. *Finding Nemo* was a lie!

For those of you teachers out there passionate about capturing and holding your students' attention (all ninety million of you), I also have good news. That data point that human attention span has slipped to 8 seconds from 12 seconds a decade prior? Also false. Weirdly, the sources of this data referenced in Microsoft's report do not actually include this data. The only reference that held a clue as to where this misinformation could have originated was a 2008 study that found the average person stays on a webpage for 12 seconds. But the study had nothing to do with attention span.

What do studies about human attention span actually say? Believe it or not, recent research reveals no material change in human attention span since the dawn of the internet and social media age.[3] You read that right: Even in our rapid, moving-a-mile-a-minute, TikToking, texting world, human attention span is holding steady. What *has* changed is our selectivity over what we give our attention to. With more information thrown at us in one day than prehistoric humans received in entire lifetimes, we must be selective about what we give our attention to, or else we'd lose our ever-loving minds.

Your students are just as capable as students in a one-room school-house—with a pencil as their novel technology tool du jour—were of remaining attentive and engaged in class. You just have to work a little smarter to capture and hold today's students' attention in the first place.

Slippery Student Attention

If it's not true that the average person has an attention span as short as 8 or even 12 seconds, then what is the average attention span, especially of students? And what does it mean about capturing their attention?

It turns out that measuring student attention isn't so black and white. In education, it's common to hear the idea that students can pay attention for as many minutes as their age. Or another common statistic is that students have attention spans of somewhere between 10 and 15 minutes. Yet like the "humans have shorter attention spans than ADHD-afflicted goldfish" theory, validation of these theories is hard to find. In 2007, psychologists Karen Wilson and James H. Korn from St. Louis University reviewed the existing research that claimed student attention taps out shortly after the ten-minute mark and found little evidence of this assertion even within the very studies purporting this number as fact. Wilson and Korn deduced that researchers failed to account for things like differences in what paying attention looks like from student to student.[4]

For example, one study they reviewed used note taking, and only note taking, as evidence of paying attention. In this study, research-ers observed that students tend to take fewer and fewer notes over the span of a lecture. The researchers took this as validation of the 10- to 15-minute attention span. But in the study itself, Wilson and Korn found no proof of a direct link between note taking and paying atten-tion, and its authors also failed to acknowledge that students could have been demonstrating attention in other ways while taking fewer notes. After all, attention can look like a lot of different things. In that banana, order of operations example in the previous chapter, attention looked like a classroom of fifth graders gawking at James as he furiously unpeeled a banana.

Wilson and Korn's meta-analysis did not lead to an average student attention span. What it did do was remind us of how very difficult it is to measure student attention and, more so, back into an average attention span.

But there's a more important fact of attention span than how long it allegedly lasts on average for students: the fact that attention waxes and wanes. In 2010, researchers from The Catholic University in Washington D.C. gave clickers to college students in entry-level physics classes. Every time students became aware that their attention had lapsed, they were directed to click one of three buttons indicating the duration of the lapse. The options were one minute or less, two to three minutes, or five minutes or more. Their responses were fed into a computer and mapped out across the class session. These maps revealed that the most frequent duration of an attention lapse was one minute or less. And these lapses occurred way more often than once every 10 or 15 minutes. Instead, researchers noticed the following typical pattern of attention lapses:

+ Attention lapse 1: Within the first 30 seconds of class
+ Attention lapse 2: Between 4.5 to 5.5 minutes into the class
+ Attention lapse 3: Between 7 to 9 minutes into the class
+ Attention lapse 4: Between 9 and 10 minutes
+ After that, attention lapses occurred more and more frequently as the class went on, but the average duration of a lapse lasting one minute or less held steady[5]

The upshot? Students may be kids, but they're not always so different from us adults. If you pause to observe your own attention lapses, you'll probably find they happen quite frequently and don't last that long. Whether we're giving our attention to something important or trivial, it starts by something getting our attention, and then eventually our attention will slip. Then we jolt back to that thing getting our attention…until it slips again, and so on. But it's not the lapse that matters. It's the ability to re-engage, to slip back into the thing that needs or wants our attention as soon as possible. For students, that's the learning. For us? The thing that needs our attention is knowing how to capture student attention and when we need to do it.

What doesn't need our attention? Trying to figure out how to hold our students' attention for every continuous second of a class. Because that's a fool's errand. Any engagement tool or strategy that promises undivided student attention across an entire class session is promising the impossible. Any tool or strategy that doesn't incorporate the reality of the fluctuations in student attention span will fall short and frustrate the teachers who attempt to use it.

The goal of the *Attention* component in *ATLAS* is to capture your students' attention and prepare them to hold it for as long as they are capable in between totally typical, expected, and momentary lapses. From there, our objective is to capture their attention again when they show signs of lapses lasting more than a few minutes. As I stated earlier, the beauty of *ATLAS* is that you do not have to use its components in order. You can toggle between and among the components to meet the

> Any engagement tool or strategy that promises undivided student attention across an entire class session is promising the impossible. Any tool or strategy that doesn't incorporate the reality of the fluctuations in student attention span will fall short and frustrate the teachers who attempt to use it.

needs of the moment your students are experiencing. Every time you sense a collective classroom or individual attention wane, you can leap back to the *Attention* component—with a pre-planned attention getter—to ignite your students' attention again and re-engage them in the learning process.

What Student Attention Means and Why It Matters

Student attention, as a defined concept, is one of those simple things that, like a number of things in education, has been made needlessly complex. Over the years, all kinds of multi-stepped, puzzle piece-like ideas and vague concepts of attention have been tossed around. The more convoluted they become, the more difficult they are to understand and implement. It's like we took this simple concept of attention and put it through a crazy Rube Goldberg machine, where it knocks over 174 dominoes, and the last one tips into some lever that causes a baseball to get propelled through a window. Then the baseball lands on a spoon handle in a cereal bowl, which triggers a catapult to spit out some crazy definition of attention. When we could have just kept its original definition.

One of the things that further complicates our understanding of student attention is that it is conflated with student engagement itself. This is justifiably confusing to teachers and also serves to confuse what student engagement means. When definitions of engagement and attention overlap, teachers don't know what to prioritize and which to pursue (attention? engagement? both? something else?), or if they must somehow pursue different goals using many of the same approaches. Further clouding this conversation is that, in an academic and cognitive sense, there are several different kinds of attention, such as processing, perceiving, filtering, active vs. passive, and so on.

When it comes to how student attention relates to engagement, let's keep it simple. Merriam-Webster's definition of *attention* most pertinent to us is "a condition of readiness for such attention involving especially a selective narrowing or focusing of consciousness and receptivity."[6] In more straightforward language, attention means we are priming our students to focus on the content and skills of the class. To achieve this, we stoke their curiosity. Curiosity is an emotional state, one that research has found motivates a person to narrow attention and participate in further exploration, as it simultaneously prepares the brain to learn and remember.[7] In this definition of attention, its goal and relationship to engagement are clear: Attention feeds into engagement. It's a precursor to and prerequisite of engagement, but engagement involves more than merely paying attention and preparing to learn. The act of capturing your students' attention, when used in conjunction with the other four *ATLAS* components, will ensure that your students have gone beyond paying attention and preparation and will progress to engaging fully in their learning. This engagement always starts with attention.

Once and for all, let's put anticipatory sets, essential questions that are not at all essential, or whatever else aside. In *ATLAS*, attention asks that you plan in advance a few moments of intrigue and curiosity to convince students that engaging in the class will be worth the time, effort, and perseverance it will require. That's it. No Rube Goldberg machine needed.

How to Capture and Hold Student Attention

In 2010, entrepreneur Derek Sivers delivered a three-minute TED Talk at a global conference. Here's how he opened his talk:

Everyone, please think of your biggest personal goal. For real. You can take a second. You've got to feel this to learn it. Take a few seconds and think of your personal biggest goal, okay? Imagine deciding right now that you're going to do it. Imagine telling someone that you meet today what you're going to do. Imagine their congratulations, and their high image of you. Doesn't it feel good to say it out loud? Don't you feel one step closer already, like it's already becoming part of your identity?[8]

In asking these questions, Sivers made the talk about his audience, not him, not his content, and not a generic idea or topic. He drew them in by asking questions that directed them to reflect on something relevant and personal and imagine what something relatable might feel like. After this opener, he goes on to surprise the audience by saying that sharing one's goals out loud makes a person less likely to achieve them. The rest of his brief talk focuses on explaining to the audience what to do instead to increase the odds of accomplishing important goals.

Let's contrast Sivers's opener to another option, a common one we all know and *don't* love. This one: "Good morning, everyone! Oh, we can do better than that—GOOD MORNING!" Such an opening to a talk not only announces to the audience that the speaker may be a wee bit combative but also that they put very little thought into the audience's experience, specifically how to cultivate their curiosity in the content to come.

The best speakers know that how they start a talk can make or break the impact and success of their entire talk. If speakers fail to pique their audience's curiosity in the critical first seconds, they will struggle to get their attention and reignite it when it naturally wanes throughout their talk. The same is true for teachers.

You can think of what you share with your students at the beginning of class as the equivalent of saying, "We're going to learn about this thing that you will find so cool and see so clearly how it impacts your life or world that you'll be willing to grapple with the concept, hang with it if you get stuck, and put effort into its comprehension and developing skills." But any storyteller worth his or her chops knows the rule "show, don't tell," so we're not going to *say* this to our students. We're going to *show* it to them through a clever, compelling opener to our classes. Like the *ATLAS* engagement formula itself, this is easier than it looks.

The first step we take will be the same for us all: Let's commit to forever parting with the sentence "Good morning/afternoon class, today we're going to learn about X thing." Try getting your students' attention with that snooze of an opener. You can almost hear their collective groan.

For our second step, you've got options. Five, in fact. To produce a list of high-impact approaches to capturing student attention, I turned to the best and most engaging speakers and relied on all I've learned as I've worked to become a better speaker myself. All told, the most effective attention getters fit into five categories: enrolling questions, stories, games/challenges, videos, and mnemonics. That's it. No need to reinvent the wheel. Those are your options. The best speakers know they have to use one of these methods to start their talks, and they come back to them a few times throughout their talks to reignite attention. But know that you do not have to turn yourself into a world-class TED talker. Nor do you have to have a banana style opener for every single lesson. Please take that to heart. Remember that our goal is simple: to stoke your students' curiosity such that they become ready and willing to participate in the learning that follows. This is achieved by planning your attention getters before class, and they need only last anywhere from a few seconds to a couple of minutes long to do their job.

> Remember that our goal is simple: to stoke your students' curiosity such that they become ready and willing to participate in the learning that follows.

The Five Ways to Capture Student Attention

Think of the attention getter as the vehicle through which we travel into students' worlds and transport them into ours; that is, to the content.

To that end, before we dive into each of the five methods, we must learn the golden rule of attention: *What you say or share in your attention getter must relate to the students, and it must relate to the content to come.*

To the extent necessary for planning a particular attention getter, "relate" can be used loosely. What matters is that there is something in the attention getter that will be familiar to your students. If you were to share a personal story from your adult life, it's likely that the average child sitting in your classroom hasn't yet experienced the details of the story in his or her life. But if you were to share something about when you were a kid, chances are your students can sufficiently relate. When students can relate to even a piece of information you share, that information can then attach to your students' existing neural pathways and be absorbed; familiar information gives the brain something to latch on to. After all, students make meaning by connecting new information to existing schema.

The content of your attention getter also doesn't have to perfectly relate to the content that will follow. Often the relationship between the attention getter and the content that follows is subtle and clarified through the transition—which we'll get into in the next chapter.

Attention Getter 1: Enrolling Questions

At its essence, Derek Sivers's TED Talk is about how broadcasting your goals to others makes you less likely to achieve them. In fact, you could say that the essential question of his TED Talk is: Does talking about your goals make you more or less likely to achieve them? But Sivers did not start with this question. Because essential questions are not actually that interesting, and they definitely aren't essential to engaging learning. Despite this fact, educators have embraced essential questions for years—and to our detriment and, worse, to our students' detriment. Sure, they might get at the heart of a debate. But they are usually theoretical and rarely personal or directly relevant to the listener. Instead,

Sivers rightly opted for an *enrolling* question.

Here's the fundamental difference: Essential questions are about our content. Enrolling questions are about our kids. Enrolling questions are those that intentionally speak to the receiver of the question; they

> Essential questions are about our content. Enrolling questions are about our kids.

are not those that are set up to speak to a concept in general. They are the difference between saying "Does talking about your goals make you more or less likely to achieve them?" and "Imagine sharing an important goal with a friend before you've set out to achieve it. How do you think that might make you feel?" Enrolling questions are personal and cause listeners to reflect on something in terms of how it relates to themselves or their worlds. They add context to content and move information from the abstract to the applicable. The point and power of an enrolling question is to make the question relevant. Because when something is framed as relevant to a listener, then that person is more likely to pay attention to the person talking and engage with the subsequent material.

Enrolling questions are naturally more engaging, relevant, and thought-provoking than essential questions, which is another reason we want to choose them over essential questions when seeking student attention. As teachers, especially if we have young children at home, it's easy to become habituated to asking very simple questions like "What's your favorite color?" Over time, we get used to questions that don't provoke thought or ask our students to use the higher order cognition that we know they need to develop. As you write your enrolling questions, do not shy away from nuance or complexity. And also do not shy away from pressing your students if they reflexively clam up in the face of a challenging question. Scaffold your challenging enrolling questions as needed and trust that by starting with a provocative question, you are priming students for participation in and perseverance through far more engaging and productive learning.

Attention Getter 2: Stories

What is more human than telling stories? In fact, there are anthropologists who believe that storytelling *is* what makes us human. For eons, humans have used storytelling to educate, learn, and strengthen bonds between individuals and among communities. Through studies that look at how storytelling shapes perception, anthropologists have found that it strongly correlates with cooperation, empathy building, and generosity. It's through story that we reflect on how we ourselves behave and feel in various circumstances, consider how we relate to others, and learn to imagine experiences through someone else's eyes. In school, stories are a powerful way to transport ourselves—across time and circumstances or out of our classrooms and into other worlds. Moreover, they don't cost a thing but can yield a hugely beneficial return.

When it comes to telling stories to capture your students' attention, be intentional. Don't tell stories for stories' sake. Tell stories that somehow link to the content to come, even if the link seems tangential. In the next chapter, we'll read how to transition from your attention getter to the lesson. If you cannot readily find the transition from your story to the learning, then it's a good sign your story's relationship to the content isn't strong enough to make sense for your students. Find any kernel from the class's content to inspire a story. If you can pinpoint their connection and articulate the transition, you've got a story that works.

I recommend outlining your story in advance of class so you're confident you've included sentences that will help your students understand and relate to the story. Just as you need not become a TED-level speaker with your enrolling questions, you also needn't write the next great American novel with your story. You simply need to have a clear beginning, middle, and end and use storytelling in a way that includes your students, makes them feel a connection to the details of the story you're sharing, and ties into the content or skills to come. If it's helpful to you, reference the story formulas we discussed in Chapter 1 to mimic their structures: the hero's journey, Freytag's Pyramid, the classic joke format, or any other story formula you find and that works for you.

Attention Getter 3: Games/Challenges

People who are experts in capturing and holding attention have been using games and challenges for a long time. Ever been to a professional baseball, basketball, or football game? You've undoubtedly seen a game or challenge during a time-out, halftime, or at a low point in the game. Think about the shell game they showed on the jumbotron, the participant they pulled from the audience to answer trivia and win a prize, or even the sausage race at Miller Park. (Baseball fans will get this reference, the rest of you can dive down a YouTube rabbit hole). Each of these are quick challenges designed to capture and recapture attention and to keep the audience engaged in what's to follow. There's a reason movie theaters show trailers before the movie begins. Attention matters, and it matters early.

Miss Curry's challenge for how fast students believed they could eat an entire banana from Chapter 2 is a perfect example of a game or challenge. However, for those of you who want to tone your creativity muscle before making up challenges of your own, technology can help. In fact, the rise of tech tools in this space—such as Kahoot, Gimkit, Quizlet, and Blooket—represents how effective games/challenges can be for capturing attention. Each of these apps shares a common goal—to engage students through game/challenge-centric modalities. The appeal to students of games or challenges is obvious. What matters is that a game or challenge directly relates to the skills and content of the class and functions as a quick gateway to more relevant content.

Attention Getter 4: Videos

All teachers have their strengths and weaknesses. When it comes to improving upon the most essential teaching skills, we must commit to doing so. But every once in a while, we all confront skills that we simply do not possess. It can be empowering and productive to recognize our limits so we can cut our losses and move on, both playing to our strengths and working to improve upon skills more accessible to us.

A few years ago, I was coaching a high school social studies teacher on this *ATLAS* work. He loved the feeling of being engrossed in a great story. Who doesn't? He decided he wanted to work on using stories to open more classes. Bless this wonderful teacher, he was just not going to be a great storyteller anytime soon. He knew it. I knew it. And we both knew it was time to move on to another attention method.

This particular teacher happened to have the most impressive knowledge of YouTube content I've ever seen. It was like he had the entire YouTube catalog stored in his brain. With such a deep understanding of how to look for and find content on YouTube that could relate to most any topic, we decided that using video clips was the strength we were going to play to in the short term as we simultaneously worked to improve his skills for other attention methods.

One day, I observed him open a class with a clip from *Da Ali G Show*, actor Sacha Baron Cohen's TV show before he started doing the Borat movies. As Ali G, Cohen played a wannabe rapper who interviewed serious people who were neither aware that Ali G was a farce nor that they were being set up for a comedy show. In the clip this teacher played, Ali G was interviewing a panel of esteemed medical experts about various ethical issues in healthcare.

At one point, in his thick cockney accent, Ali G asks them, "Does they [doctors] have the right to end old people's lives?"

A doctor responds, "That's euthanasia."

Ali G says, "Why is it the responsibility of the youth in Asia for killing someone else? Surely it's between that patient and the doctor."[9]

What follows is a dialogue between Ali G and the doctors in which he continues to conflate "youth in Asia" with "euthanasia," and the perplexed doctors take turns trying to explain to him that the youth in Asia are not responsible for making euthanasia decisions. Of course, to see it written, the confusion is obvious. But to hear it—especially in Baron Cohen's masterful deadpan—is the joke. As the students watched, some understood the joke, others didn't. Once the clip was over, the teacher explained it, to a laugh from the class.

This teacher's use of the clip was perfect. He used it to transition to an excellent modified Socratic seminar about the ethics of euthanasia and who, if not the youth in Asia, is responsible for decisions of its legality and use. Video clips can work in numerous ways. In this case, the teacher took a clip of a show that was popular among his students at the time and leveraged its comedy as a point of connection. By sharing in laughter, the entire class was able to get on the same page at the start of the class. Furthermore, comedy helped ease the students out of some discomfort around discussing sensitive and complicated subject matter.

That said, not all clips used in class need to be comedy. Not by any stretch. What matters when selecting videos is that they include some detail that will resonate with your students and link, if even in a small way, to the content. Such details could be something topical to your students' lives, an actor or personality people their age know of and enjoy, a popular song, or anything else you're aware of that your students care about or are interested in. Bear in mind that a totally irrelevant video can be an attention repellent.

The caveat of videos is that sometimes teachers use them too often and begin to rely on videos to do the attention getting *and* teaching instead of them. As a rule of thumb, only use videos if you are certain a video will succeed in getting your students' attention and that you can make a logical transition from the video to the learning to come. If you find you are using video to outsource a bit of teaching, that's a good sign you might be better off with a different attention getter.

Attention Getter 5: Mnemonics

In Chapter 1, I shared the story of Mark Essay, a mentor of mine and educator at the academic summer camp, who used the hours of a clock face to help students learn and memorize the first twelve elements on the periodic table of elements. He matched the hour to the element's placement in the table and created a little story around its elemental symbol. For each, he used memorable gestures, keywords, and also moved around the clock. In other words, he used all kinds of mnemonics. Had Mark used only one of these tools, it would have been impressive. But he managed to use three types of mnemonics in one attention getter!

Mnemonics are any tool or trick designed to aid in memory and retention. Many of them lend to curiosity-stoking openers to a class session. Examples of mnemonics that can make for effective attention getters include:

- *Imagery and Visualization*: Mark's clock face was this kind of mnemonic device. He used physical location on an imaginary clock to anchor each element to a time on the clock that represented their order on the periodic table of elements.
- *Keyword Method*: In this mnemonic, a series of words is used and repeated to help an audience remember a different but similar sounding word. Integral to the success of this method in aiding memory is attaching it to some mental image. Mark did this beautifully for several of the elements. For *hydrogen*, he used "hide your gems" along with the image of his girlfriend walking into the jewelry store when he was there on a secret mission to buy her an engagement ring.

+ *Total Physical Response (TPR)*: TPR uses physical movements to make connections to words, phrases, or sentences. Mark folded TPR into several of his element stories. When he repeated "hide your gems," he asked everyone to put their imaginary gems into their pockets.

As you experiment with using mnemonics to capture student attention, do some online research and have some fun. There are many more kinds of mnemonics than I list here. There are also subject area mnemonics that are worth googling for ideas if relevant to you. Some mnemonics, such as acronyms, acrostics, and the Method of Loci, lend themselves much more to memory and retention tools than to attention getters. But you are limited only by your imagination.

What Attention Looks Like

Starting every class with one of these five attention getters is an integral part of *ATLAS*. So is returning to them when you see that students are not paying close attention. Recall that most attention lapses last about a minute or less. Particularly as students age and mature, they will become better at returning to attention on their own. It's the lapses that appear to drag on into minutes that demand we use one of the five attention getters to draw them back in. So we must become aware of how students indicate their attention to learning so we can recognize its absence.

When students are paying attention, you will see:

+ Students appear alert and are tracking you, classmates, or any visuals with their eyes
+ Students are taking notes
+ Students are listening to you or classmates as opposed to talking (when they're not supposed to be talking), sleeping, or being on phones when phones must be put away

- Students are asking or responding to questions
- Students are following requests you or their classmates have made of them
- Students are reacting to discussion and learning with feelings or emotions, e.g., laughing, showing excitement, demonstrating frustration, conveying confusion, and so on

Best Practices of the Five Attention Getters

- Always follow the golden rule of attention: Whatever you say or share in your attention getter must relate to the students, and it must relate to the content to come.
- Plan your attention getters before every class. Where helpful and relevant, outline them, if even in a rough bullet point form, and rehearse them a few times before class.
- Early in your *ATLAS* work, identify which one or two of the five attention getter methods are most natural to you. If helpful in assessing your strengths, ask a colleague for his or her feedback and opinion. Play to your strengths. Doing so makes *ATLAS* much more gratifying for you and much more effective for your students. That said, always work to develop attention getters that feel more challenging to you.
- The goal is to feel confident using as many of these attention getters as possible so that you can rotate them regularly. They will all retain their power to captivate students if they are not used in every class but are instead used intermittently.
- Whenever and wherever possible, make the attention getter about your students. Personalize it, and demonstrate how it's relevant to them. I say whenever and wherever possible because some attention getters, like enrolling questions and games/challenges, lend themselves more naturally to being directly about

your students. Videos will likely be the hardest to consistently involve your students. Yet if you keep this objective front and center as you search for the best attention getters to match content and skills, you will be much more likely to find or frame them to be about your students in some way.

Best Practices for Re-Capturing Attention

It's a guarantee that you will use an attention getter to start your class. However, have a handful ready to go in advance of class to use when you identify attention lapses that last more than two or three minutes (i.e., notice an absence of indicators of attention listed in the prior section). Note that you can use attention getters for the entire class, groups (when students are engaged in group work), or individual students.

While all five attention getters work well for the start of class, some lend themselves more naturally to use in the middle of class. Enrolling questions, videos, and certain categories of mnemonics will be the most likely to lend themselves to quick and lightweight attention getters throughout class. And, as we'll see in Chapter 5 on the Lesson component, quick formative assessments are also a great way to recapture attention. My general rule is use what makes the most sense based on the content, your desired learning outcomes, and flow of the class. Bear in mind that while reigniting your students' attention throughout class is vital to ensuring they learn, there's a little less pressure on how you approach mid-class attention getters. Convincing your students that what they'll learn in a given class is worth their engagement is a heavier lift than asking them to come back to learning you'd already convinced them was worth their time and effort. Plan your mid-class attention getters—and put more thought and energy into how you will open your class.

Always strive to shore up your skills for all attention getters so you can rotate them consistently at the start of class. But you might be pleased to know that research suggests it's OK to lean more heavily on questions to reignite attention throughout class. This is especially true during lectures. From the same Catholic University study in which students used a clicker to indicate an attention lapse, data revealed fewer reported lapses in attention during lecture segments in the time immediately following a question.[10] In other words, asking a question during a lecture gets a student attention bump. As often as you can, aim for enrolling questions, but know that essential questions and questions designed to check for comprehension also work to recapture attention throughout class.

CHAPTER 4

Transition

When my daughter, Charlotte, was little, she refused to go into the ocean. Her fear? Not the water, not sharks, not the waves, not undertow. Seaweed. She found it slimy and "gross." And you know what? She's not wrong. Seaweed does have a way of sneaking up on you and creepily brushing your leg with its weirdly slippery tentacles. But that's no reason not to have fun splashing around in the ocean. Especially when Charlotte's brother, Everett, was doing just that while she remained planted firmly on dry ground and missing out.

When in doubt, trick your kids! In a good way, of course. The way that promotes a little healthy risk taking and growth. Molly and I decided to try out a strategy where we used the lure of finding seashells to coax Charlotte into the water, where, we explained dubiously, the "better" shells were. We were able to convince her to walk to the water's edge, where no slimy seaweed could sneak up on her. Then we'd challenge her to find a black shell, or a sand dollar, or a shell with both its halves still attached. We told her that the deeper she went into the ocean, the more shell variety she'd see. (Never mind that the odds of finding shells when more immersed in water than not is unlikely... Tricks are for kids!) We repeated this cycle—issue a challenge and nudge her to walk a bit deeper into the water to explore. So fixated on finding the shell we described and so excited when she did, Charlotte followed us a little deeper into the ocean, and a little deeper—until, before she knew it, she was waist deep.

"Charlotte, look at you!" Molly said. "The water is up to your waist! What do you think, is it possible to be in the ocean and not have to touch too much seaweed?"

Charlotte was scouring for seashells so intently that she hadn't realized how far into enemy territory she'd gone. She looked up, visibly surprised to be so deep in the ocean. Before she could panic or run back to the dry sand, I encouraged her to come a bit farther into the water to see what else we might find.

"I think you have learned that you can be in the ocean without seaweed stopping your fun!" I said. "Whad'ya say we walk a bit further out to meet your brother and explore the ocean more," I said as I pointed to Everett a few feet in front of us. Little Charlotte bravely marched into the water and began splashing around with abandon and joy. Never did a scary, slimy seaweed nest float our way.

It would be some years before Charlotte outgrew her seaweed aversion entirely. In fact, the phobia still rears its ugly head from time to time. But on that day, she learned a surprising lesson. She learned she could share space with seaweed and still have fun.

As is obvious by now, I love surprising people with learning. As a parent, a teacher, and a coach, I love providing learning experiences that are not initially identifiable as explicit lessons. When I was a kid, I was always delighted when someone could surprise me with learning, especially in school. To discover that a fascinating story, an intriguing experience, or a fun activity was, in fact, learning was akin to uncovering a treat after the best kind of trick—one where learning was hidden in information that spoke to my personal interests, stoked my curiosity, or even just made me smile or laugh. Such surprise learning always felt like a reprieve from the boring, didactic teaching style many of my teachers seemed to have. For children, some of the best learning happens when kids don't realize it's happening.

It would take some time before I developed the skill of "trick" or "surprise" learning to a point where I was confident enough to use it

For children, some of the best learning happens when kids don't realize it's happening.

daily in class, much less teach it to others. Although I knew I liked surprise learning, I was initially clueless as to how to make it happen. That's an understatement. Any *Bold Schoolers* out there know my most humiliating student teaching moment, which I—boldly, if I may say so—admitted in *Bold School*. Back when I was in college, I had been asked to student-teach a history class on President Teddy Roosevelt. I rounded up a selection of items that could represent the things for which Roosevelt is most remembered. A fake tree for his conservation efforts. A cowboy on a horse figurine for the Rough Riders. Part of a tree stump for big stick diplomacy. I got to the classroom before students had arrived to put the assorted crap—let's call a spade a spade—on a table at the front of the room. And then, well, I covered it all in a bed sheet—so that I could do a big reveal and "surprise" students with the key points of Roosevelt's presidency we'd be discussing that day. Turns out, this is not surprise learning. Nor is it learning at all. It is just a bed sheet over some junk that means nothing to no one and is interesting to exactly zero humans.

My instinct to start class with some sort of surprising twist wasn't wrong—my execution was. The element of surprise in learning—or merging information or actions that in some way feels incongruent—can function as a sort of cognitive reset that motivates greater focus on the new information that follows the surprise.[1] Thankfully, I'd eventually meet Mark Essay, creator of the imaginary clock face mnemonic for the first twelve periodic table elements and master of crafting surprising twists in learning. When I saw him in action, I thought, *Now, that's how it's done!* He was integral to helping me think through how to surprise kids into learning. He helped teach me the art and science of opening class in a way that brought students to your side in a desire to engage in learning, not in a way that would induce narcolepsy.

Inspired by how I liked being subtly tricked into learning as a student, applying what Mark Essay taught me, and fine-tuning the art and science of surprise learning over the years, I arrived at the attention getters we discussed in the prior chapter. In time, I also came to understand what was happening in students' brains when they were experiencing surprise learning and how it must be leveraged to lead to deep learning.

Laying the Schematic Groundwork

In 2019, educators Jal Mehta and Sarah Fine published *In Search of Deeper Learning: The Quest to Remake the American High School.* In their book, they shared what they gleaned from some of America's most innovative schools. Of course, innovation is only useful if it achieves educators' main goal—getting students to learn deeply and learn to see how different knowledge domains interrelate, such that students can nimbly apply skills to a range of areas. About deep learning, Mehta and Fine write:

> ...what does it mean to understand something deeply? Cognitive scientists think of deep learning—or what they might call "learning for understanding"—as the ability to organize discrete pieces of knowledge into a larger schema of understanding. Research suggests that deep learners have schemas that enable them to see how discrete pieces of knowledge in a domain are connected; rather than seeing isolated facts, they see patterns and connections because they understand the underlying structures of the domain they are exploring...A related idea is that deep

understanding allows you to transfer knowledge—not only to use it in the context in which it was taught, but also to understand or explain something in a related context.[2]

As we know, the *ATLAS* model positions us to open every class in a way that captures our students' attention with information that relates to them and the content to come, even if the relationships aren't immediately obvious to students. That is the golden rule of the *Attention* component, and it's highly intentional. Attention getter information that relates, if even in a small way, to students' lives, interests, or shared experiences will not only capture their attention, but it will also help them make meaning of new content and prepare them for understanding. Relatable information has an existing neural pathway, or knowledge context, to latch onto for comprehension, or even partial comprehension for now. In other words, the information can be plugged into an existing schema.

Schema is defined as "a structured framework or plan."[3] As it relates to cognition, *schema* is further defined as "a mental codification of experience that includes a particular organized way of perceiving cognitively and responding to a complex situation or set of stimuli."[4] In layman's terms, *schema* refers to a mental and conceptual framework through which we perceive, understand, and respond to information.

In super simplified terms, think of the brain like a closet. The clothing racks are the brain's inherent wiring. Schemata act as hangers that get hung on the racks over time to support clothes, the new ideas or information that are hung over the course of a life. Without the hangers, the clothes have no place to go. Without schema, new ideas will simply float around untethered in a person's brain, with no context to which the ideas can latch onto for meaning-making. And students can only make meaning by connecting the new ideas to an existing schema.

The ability to bridge from an existing schema to a new one allows us to understand new information in a broader context. From there, we can engage with that information, steadily deepen our understanding of it, and take more action with it. If we confront information for which we have no existing schema, we cannot understand that information—and we will not understand that information until someone or something provides a data point we already know that we can leverage to build a new schema and enable and support comprehension. By definition, this means that a new schema is always born from an existing schema.

By opening class with information familiar to our students, we are giving them an existing schema to work with throughout class. Not only are we starting class in a way that piques their curiosity, but we are also using recognizable information to *show* students they have the existing cognitive capacity to handle the learning to come. This is key. If we start class with totally unknown information, it's the equivalent of shutting the door in students' faces—particularly students with low confidence and low self-efficacy. Familiar information is the equivalent of an open door to learning. It allows students to believe they know enough to be able to engage in and overcome even the most challenging of learning moments. This is how we shore up their confidence and promote their self-efficacy over time.

> Familiar information is the equivalent of an open door to learning.

Familiar information also provides students with a known data point so that throughout the lesson they will be able "to see how discrete pieces of knowledge in a domain are connected," as Mehta and Fine say[5]. By offering a point of information connectivity in the attention getter, we are laying the groundwork for students to make ongoing connections with the lesson content. We are, then, priming them for deep learning.

We are also priming students to make connections across seemingly disconnected domains. This is where the "surprise" element of the attention getter plays an even higher-level role. The five attention getters set you up to deliver surprise learning. They guide you to be creative and use information that doesn't necessarily have a fully overlapping or obvious relationship to the lesson content. When you link the information of the attention getter to the lesson of the day with an intentional transitional phrase, you are showing your students a surprising connection between seemingly unrelated information. You are modeling the transfer of knowledge that Mehta and Fine identify as a second indicator of deep learning. When students grasp that they can transfer knowledge, they create the opening to, ever more nimbly, apply knowledge to various contexts and domains. They become deep learners capable of eventually achieving and maintaining deep learning on their own.

To drive home understanding of this concept, let's attach it to an existing schema. Let's return to the order of operations banana example from Chapter 2. Recall that Miss Curry challenged her sixth graders as to who could eat an entire banana the fastest. Using the games/challenges attention getter, Miss Curry wove in an experience that any sixth grader would know well—eating a banana. (That is how simple it can be to find relatable information for your attention getter.) She would go on to connect this familiar experience to the content of the lesson—order of operations. By the end of class, students understood that order of operations plays a critical role in arithmetic. And they also grasped that it has relevance in a multitude of contexts, such as eating a banana, that they were now empowered to ponder.

Drawing this kind of knowledge transfer out, we can see infinite instances in which order of operations is relevant. It's relevant to how a mechanical engineer who designs car engines would think through the order of operations of the steps an engine must go through to start and start safely. It's relevant to how a chef might design the steps of a recipe, optimizing both for time and achieving the intended chemical reactions in the right order when certain ingredients are combined.

The more schemata we can help students create and begin to see as related in some way, the more we can help them learn to create new schemata on their own. And the more we can empower them to be life-long deep learners, capable of connecting all kinds of disparate-seeming dots and capable of always developing new skills and seeing opportunities to apply them to different paradigms and settings. All of this schematic alchemy is a function of bridging one schema to another.

Transitions: The Schematic Bridge

When Miss Curry gave the, "On your mark, get set, go" to James, he began peeling the banana. After which, she interrupted him to ask why he was peeling the banana. After all, she challenged him to eat the *entire* banana. Once James grasped the literalness of the challenge, Miss Curry confirmed with him his belief that "order matters."

Then came her transition: "That's right, class. *Order matters,*" she said. "That's why, today, we're going to learn all about order of operations and why it matters."

With this, class was off to the races. Or at least off to the lesson. In two brief sentences, Miss Curry had masterfully distilled the common link between the attention-getter content and content to come ("order matters") and labeled the skill/academic concept that would be the focus of the class (order of operations). In doing so, she was able to achieve the ultimate goal of the transitional phrase that pays—bridging her students' existing schema to the new schema to begin understanding the information that will be delivered in the lesson.

Put more directly, the bridge is the distillation of connectivity between attention getter and new learning and labeling of the skill/academic concept. It is through this execution—and only this execution—of the transition that it can sufficiently establish the necessary connection and forward movement away from the *Attention* component of class and onto the *Lesson* component. Without explicitly articulating the connective tissue of new and upcoming information and naming the skill/concept, you risk leaving the two schemata disconnected as you head into the lesson. In turn, this risks confusing students and sty-mieing their ability to engage in class and learn the content deeply–or at all.

Keep in mind that brevity matters for student comprehension here, too. While transitions can be a few words, a sentence, or a few sentences, know that the more concise they are, the easier it is for students to cull from them the connection and concept they need to hold onto and carry with them into the lesson.

Hopefully by now, why we articulate the connective tissue and label the skill/academic concept *after* the attention getter makes sense: Surprise learning can only happen if the experience comes before the explicit connection and label. Too often, teachers articulate these points before the experience, rendering a surprise impossible and boredom likely. If Miss Curry had started her class with "Today, we're going to talk about order of oper-ations" before launching into the banana challenge, not only would she have lost most students, but she also would have introduced them to an unfamiliar term with no exist-ing schema to bridge to this new term. Or, for students who might have already been familiar with order of operations, she would have spoiled the surprise of the banana challenge entirely. Instead, she correctly first provided an experience revealing the importance of order of operations in a real-world example and then bridged students to the new mathe-matical concept of order of operations.

> Surprise learning can only happen if the experience comes before the explicit connection and label.

Another way to think of transitions is that they tell students that they just experienced surprise learning. They are the surprise Char-lotte felt when Molly and I pointed out that she was waist deep in the water. They are a plot twist. They are the big reveal—except not in the removal of a sheet-hiding-some-crap sort of way. Instead, it happens in a way that what you uncover for students is a new academic concept for which they've already been shown some real-world relevance and application.

Surprise learning and schematic bridging cannot happen without the *Transition* component of *ATLAS*. Transitions are not throwaway sentences or words. They are the phrase that pays. They are the distillation of your entire lesson into a single sentence. Don't let their brevity—or the length of this chapter—fool you. Transitions give meaning to your attention getter, to which you put in so much time and creativity to craft. Without a transition, the attention getter's potential is squandered.

A Transition Trick of the Trade

Recall Derek Sivers's TED Talk from the last chapter? The entrepreneur who spoke about how sharing your goals out loud makes you less likely to achieve them? To refresh your memory, here's how he used enrolling questions to open his talk:

> Everyone, please think of your biggest personal goal. For real. You can take a second. You've got to feel this to learn it. Take a few seconds and think of your personal biggest goal, okay? Imagine deciding right now that you're going to do it. Imagine telling someone that you meet today what you're going to do. Imagine their congratulations, and their high image of you. Doesn't it feel good to say it out loud? Don't you feel one step closer already, like it's already becoming part of your identity?

Now that we understand the power and point of the transition, I will share Sivers's transition moment with you here: "Well, bad news. You should have kept your mouth shut. Because that good feeling now will make you less likely to do it. Repeated psychology tests have proven that telling someone your goal makes it less likely to happen."[6]

In that moment there, Sivers bridged his audience from the familiar experience of excitedly sharing one's goals to the new knowledge about how detrimental this can be to achieving goals. He then moves on to explain the research that validates his claim about sharing goals and what to do instead to make them more likely to come to fruition.

There's something else worth calling out from Sivers's talk. He used a device that great speakers know will signal that something important is being said: repetition. Leading into his transition moment, Sivers starts three statements with the word "Imagine." Repetition can come in many forms. Sivers happened to use the repetition device *anaphora*, which is derived from Greek words meaning to carry or reference back. As a rhetorical device, *anaphora* is "repetition of a word or expression at the beginning of successive phrases, clauses, sentences, or verses especially for rhetorical or poetic effect."[7] Anaphora's opposite, *epistrophe*, uses the same kind of word repetition but at the end of a sentence or phrase. There's also *alliteration*, which is the repetition of certain sounds or consonance in neighboring words or syllables. Repetition of any form can lead to a few different effects, but it always stresses the importance of the words that surround it.

We often see repetition in the most famous speeches. For example, in Martin Luther King, Jr.'s "I Have a Dream" speech. King gave this transcendent speech at the 1963 March on Washington, where 250,000 mostly Black Americans marched in solidarity to demand equality under the law. In his speech, King used the "I have a dream" sentence structure eight times in close succession. Winston Churchill's "We Shall Fight on the Beaches" speech is another example. Churchill gave his rousing call to arms in June 1940 to the British House of Commons. This was in the early days of WWII, when the prime minister had come to understand that the Nazi threat could be ignored no longer. At the end of his speech, he used the "we shall fight" clause structure eight times.

In both of their speeches, King and Churchill used repetition to drive home their emphatic resolve and beliefs. They also both used it to serve two additional and important goals—persuasion and memory. King was trying to persuade listeners to share in his dream for Black Americans. Churchill was trying to persuade the House of Commons to back the United Kingdom's entry into war. Imagine how much less persuasive one sentence that starts with "I have a dream" or "We will fight" would have been. Both men were also—intentionally, we can assume—providing memorable phrases that the audience's brains could latch onto in order to retain the thesis or point behind the repeated words. Not only do we remember King's "I have a dream" phrase all these decades later, but we also remember specifics of that dream even though we (likely) don't remember his speech verbatim.

Repetition can be a powerful tool to use as you lead your students to and through the transition moment. This is not to say you have to use it with the same artfulness and brilliance that speakers like King and Churchill could. Of course not! But when you use repetition, you will likely achieve three things: 1) Signal to your students to pay close attention, as something important is happening or being said. 2) Persuade them to listen and consider a point. 3) Help them remember the point or concept surrounding the repeated words.

This is precisely what Miss Curry did. Three sentences that preceded her transition included, in slightly varied form, language along the lines of "So, James thinks he can eat an entire banana in seven seconds." She also began peppering in the words "order" and "matters" to her questions. By repeating the question and the words that captured the essence of that day's class, she was telling her students that something important was happening, and she was priming their brains to remember. Within moments—when she could all but guarantee that every student in her class was paying close attention—she bridged the connection between the banana and order of operations.

With that, Miss Curry had created the perfect sales pitch and optimal cognitive circumstances for students to *opt into* engaging in the lesson.

Best Practices of Transitions

- Script your transition phrase, sentence, or moment. While you can get away with outlining your attention getter, I recommend teachers script their transitions. Especially in the early days of practicing the *Transition* component, as it is so important to your students' capacity to engage with and deeply learn the lesson content.
- Explicitly articulate the essence of the learning and label the skill or concept of the lesson in your transition. Remember that the summarizing distillation and the label are the bridge from old to new schemata; therefore, the distillation and the label must always come *after* the old schema has been made known to students through your attention getter.
- Make your transition as concise as possible so that the skill or concept label is obvious and easier for students to remember.
- Use repetition in any form to lead into your transition when possible. It's not necessary, but it can increase the impact of your transition moment.

CHAPTER 5

Lesson

Molly and I have grown close with the pastor at our church. One evening, we'd invited Father Matt to our house for dinner. I was telling him that I was in the process of writing this very book. This led to a conversation about what's known as the "forgetting curve," which is the summation of research capturing how rapidly people forget new information, especially without any immediate effort to boost retention. Matt remarked that he was constantly struck by how few parishioners remembered the most important messages of his homily, even just an hour after he delivered it to them.

For those of you who aren't church-goers, the homily is when the deacon, pastor, or priest reflects on a Bible passage read pretty early in the service. When it comes to feedback on their "speeches," priests—and pastors, rabbis, preachers, and the like across religions—are in a unique position. After a service, priests will often stand at the exit and chat and shake hands with congregants as they leave. Usually, people will thank them for their wise words and share what resonated with them most. Not surprisingly, parishioners are often effusive with praise for their pastor. Who wants to offend or criticize people with a direct line into heaven! Those who deliver homilies and sermons get an unusually high volume of feedback—and it's totally biased and very unlikely to include constructive criticism. This perpetuates a cycle where too few ministers work on their public speaking skills, or even consider that they could benefit from doing so.

As anyone who's heard me speak about education knows, I talk often about how lousy we humans are at assessing ourselves. Plenty of research confirms that we lack the distance to objectively observe and perceive ourselves. It turns out that priests, pastors, rabbis, and all clergy are just like us. They, too, struggle with assessment, in this case of their homilies and sermons. They have the added confusion of streams of people pouring compliments on them after the service. At least we educators never have to worry about our students' incessant praise of our performance after class, right?

To Father Matt's great credit, because so many parishioners weren't remembering the points from his homily he wanted them to remember, it occurred to him that perhaps there was room for improvement in how he crafted homilies. I asked if he'd like me to workshop some homilies with him. As someone who keynotes in school districts and at conferences, I've had no choice but to learn the art and science of public speaking to level up my game. Father Matt knows what I do for a living, so he took me up on my offer.

To get us started, I asked what he wanted people to take away from the homily we were outlining. He listed about ten points—for what is typically about a twelve-minute talk. That comes to nearly one important point he wants people to retain per minute. But the fact is, our brains simply cannot retain this much information in so little time. I asked him to prioritize what was truly most important. His response was the classic answer teachers also give when I ask them to prioritize content for a given lesson. Father Matt said, "Everything's important!"

I don't fault him, or any teacher for that matter, for this response. In his view, people's souls are on the line when it comes to drawing lessons from services. But these souls remain firmly affixed to a very human brain with very real limits. If Father Matt wanted his congregants to learn from church, he was going to have to speak to the brain to get to the soul.

As business and management expert Patrick Lencioni famously said, "If everything is important, then nothing is." This was the heart of Father Matt's challenge—he was constructing homilies without prioritized information presented hierarchically. In the absence of key themes or points intentionally driven home, parishioners were left to decide for themselves what was important. Naturally, this was based on whatever felt most familiar to them, which was often something totally different from what the pastor wanted them to hold onto.

What Father Matt had not incorporated into his homily was the fact of the forgetting curve and all its surrounding implications. This is what teachers almost always forget—no pun intended—to factor into their lesson plans, as well. Human memory is fallible. Except, thanks to recent neuroscience, we're learning that this is largely by design and even a good thing. In fact, in the transference of knowledge to students, we can use their perfectly human and forgetful brains to our advantage. We can work to amplify their successful retention of what is most critical that they learn by guiding them to infer what they can forget.

The Forgetting Curve

The time between the homily and when parishioners file out and share their remarks with the priest is, at least in Catholic services, around an hour. This time lapse alone guarantees meaningful memory loss. If people were delivered information in a way that lacked hierarchy within that hour of time? Then all bets are off. It's anyone's guess what people will remember and why.

It's easy to assume that when people forget something, it's due to some failing or flaw on their part. It's also easy to beat ourselves up for not remembering things we thought we wanted to retain. Well, I've got good news for you. Neuroscience suggests that our memories are always trying to work to our advantage—even when they forget.

Imagine that you could remember every single moment of your life in exhaustive detail. There are people with such superhuman memories, many of whom mention that it can be a burden. The fading of painful experiences over time, for one, enables us to heal wounds and maintain forward momentum in our lives. Superhuman memories can also impede the cognitive process of making meaning of things. In 1968, A.R. Luria, a Russian clinical neuropsychologist, wrote of "Patient S.," a research subject of his who could forget things only with proactive, persistent effort.[1] While retention of everything was automatic for S., Luria observed that his memory lacked flexibility. For one, S. struggled to make generalizations from his experiences, a process that requires "pruning" certain details from our memories in order to coalesce the more salient or related points around some sort of unifying concept. If every single detail of every single moment is retained, information cannot be organized into hierarchy in order to make meaning of experiences. Only through the act of forgetting can the significant points bubble up in the brain and feed meaning-making and memory.

When considered in this way, forgetting is a boon. When we forget, we are pruning our brains of data deemed unimportant and freeing up space for higher-order thinking. In 2017, neurobiologists Blake Richards and Paul Frankland published a meta-analysis of new research inspecting the "transience" of memory—or forgetting, in layman's terms. Until recently, most research about memory has focused on the role remembering, or "persistence," plays in memory. In the persistence view of memory, forgetting is seen as the villain that undermines

> When we forget, we are pruning our brains of data deemed unimportant and freeing up space for higher-order thinking.

retention. With newer studies inspecting the purpose of forgetting, our general understanding of how memory works is beginning to shift. Specifically, forgetting is getting a bit of a reputation rehabilitation.

What Richards and Frankland concluded from their research was that forgetting is an evolutionary strategy designed to help humans optimize decision-making and survival.[2] Persistence (remembering) and transience (forgetting) work in tandem to help the brain prune less valuable information as a mechanism to retain more valuable information. This catalyzes the ability to make generalizations and take action. Let's think through how this might have played out when prehistoric humans were wandering the earth. Imagine a primitive human, with a super-*sapiens* memory that couldn't forget, migrating in search of a milder climate. Given that this nomad retained every tiny detail of every environment he'd experienced, he would struggle to parse the important data points, like access to water or safely edible plants nearby, from the irrelevant. If every factor, no matter how insignificant, remains of equal status in his decision-making process, he would be paralyzed in trying to distill his observations into generalizations or patterns about the habitability of this new environment. Again, if everything is important, nothing is.

Every human who's walked a younger child into a toy store for the first time has seen a version of this decision paralysis. Imagine that every toy lining the shelves represents something that could be of value to this youngster—that is, something that could provide moments of intoxicating fun, no matter how fleeting. It makes sense that toy stores can break children's brains. How can a little kid possibly choose amongst thousands of toys if she believes that all could potentially be fun? If all toys are important, then none actually is. The difference is that, in the typically forgetful brain, as kids age, they learn which toys they tend to prefer and forget those they don't, making deciding which toy to grab a more manageable process.

Forgetting allows our brains to reduce the noise of less relevant data so that we can remember the important data. From there, we can make generalizations, see themes and patterns, draw conclusions, make more informed decisions, and take decisive action. As we learn and retain more, we bring that much more context with us when we confront new information, such that the decisions we make and the actions we take will be better informed. Forgetting lets us function with prioritized information rather than remaining paralyzed by the sum of all information's weight.

The good news here is that most of us don't have super-human brains that retain every millisecond of our lives in perfect detail. Yet the reality remains that there are plenty of moments in life—such as in school, at work, in important relationships—where it's to our benefit to actively try to retain certain information. And, as neuroscience shows us, how and when we work to retain new information is critical. Because unless actress Marilu Henner (who's revealed she can even remember her baptism as a baby!) is reading this book, all our brains are going to forget at least some new information, no matter what—and, as it turns out, pretty darn quickly.

This is where the forgetting curve comes in. In 1885, German psychologist Hermann Ebbinghaus wanted to understand why humans forget and what, if anything, we could do to promote retention. The fruits of his research produced the famous forgetting curve (figure 1), which captures how memory is a function of time, with the greatest memory loss happening within the first hour after exposure to information. When someone is exposed to new information, it goes into their short-term memory. Only through proactive steps can this information move into a person's long-term memory. Without intervention, the average person will forget 56 percent of the information they were just exposed to in one hour.[3] Twenty-four hours later, that will jump by ten percentage points to 66 percent of the information having been forgotten. Assuming a person continues to take no steps to promote retention, after six days, 75 percent of the information will be wiped from a person's memory. In case anyone is dubious about research born of an era when people were still traveling by horse and buggy (or an era when people didn't have 24/7 internet access to look up information), scientists replicated Ebbinghaus's research in 2015, which validated the forgetting curve.[4]

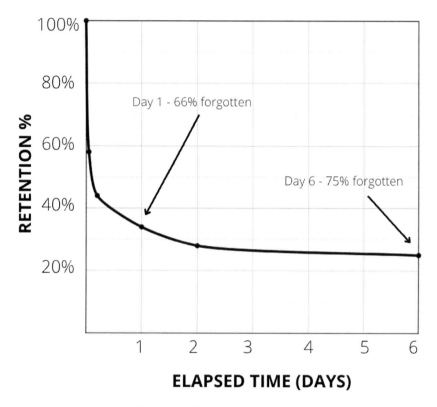

Figure 1. The Forgetting Curve

Ebbinghaus drew some additional key conclusions from his research.[5] For example, it's much easier for people to remember things that have some meaning or relevance to them. As we discussed in the prior chapter, tons of research since Ebbinghaus's day has reaffirmed this observation. Information that can attach, if even only tangentially, to preexisting schema in our brains stands a stronger chance of having meaning to us, and meaning promotes memory.

Perhaps Ebbinghaus's most important finding on memory, at least as it pertains to us educators, is that how information is presented to a person directly impacts that person's ability to understand and retain it. Herein lies the great news for teachers.

Up to this point in the *ATLAS* model, we have captured our students' attention and used a transition moment to bridge new information to a schema our students already have. We have given the new data some meaning for them to latch onto as we move them into the lesson. We have thus teed them up to understand this information. From here, we have the ability to present the lesson's information in a way that optimizes the likelihood students will understand and retain the most salient points of the content. For us teachers, the question we must be aware of is: How do our students' brains determine what's important and what's not? How do they know what they can forget in order to prioritize what needs to be remembered? The answer? Us.

Our Role—and Power—in Influencing Our Students' Memories

Let's be honest for a moment. Let's take a page from Father Matt and confront the role we might be playing in what our students remember and forget from our lessons. Because here's the thing—it's human nature to hold learners of information entirely responsible for forgetting pieces of it. That they play a role is unequivocally true; memory is a function of forgetting *and* proactive and intentional retention. However, the deliverers of information hold meaningful power in guiding receivers as to what they can discard and what they need to focus on working to retain. In fact, as teachers transferring information to students, we hold more influence over what our students remember than they do.

When Father Matt and I workshopped his homilies, I suggested he whittle down the content of each to one or two critical points. Then we'd work to structure the homilies in a way that made these two points obvious and ensured they were repeated a few times. As if by miracle—or just best practice of public speaking pros—parishioners, including myself, were remembering more of what Father Matt hoped we would. With each hand shaken and conversation had with congregants upon exit, Father Matt was getting authentic validation of the power of prioritizing key information for those receiving it. That parishioners were leaving with the takeaway Father Matt intended also proved that they were listening to and engaged in his homily. Without a doubt, every single one of us sitting in church experienced multiple momentary attention lapses when he spoke—after all, we are human, and that's what the human mind does. But because Father Matt reiterated the priority points throughout his homily, we were able to absorb them despite our briefly wandering minds.

We have the power to do the exact same thing—to craft lessons optimized for our students' memory. To build them in a way that actually helps students know what they can forget so that they may more readily remember what you want them to retain. And to design them to ensure that students remain engaged in the lesson, inevitable attention lapses and all. It's a matter of prioritization and information hierarchy.

Prioritizing Content—For the Year

In the *ATLAS* model, the *Lesson* component refers to the period of class where we transfer information and knowledge to students. We typically do this by lecture, video/audio/podcast clips, and/or close read. And, as you now understand, we're going to present information hierarchically so it's optimized for retention.

As part of planning each lesson, you will identify and prioritize the most important ideas you want students to remember. But this work doesn't begin when you sit down to plan the week's upcoming lessons. This work of prioritizing content starts in the summer.

Every teacher knows that content standards are too many and too unrealistic to teach in a year. Trying to cover all of them forces us to jam too much content into every lesson, such that we risk overwhelming students with way more information than their brains could reasonably be expected to retain. Furthermore, trying to cover all standards makes it near impossible for us to identify the most critical points around which to anchor our lessons. Have I mentioned that if everything is important, nothing is?

Whenever possible, I highly recommend that you meet on a schedule with fellow grade-level teachers to prioritize content standards. It's wise to begin this work in the summer. Together, you can help each other whittle down all standards to a manageable number you agree to focus on and help each other reinforce throughout the year. You can meet quarterly, monthly, every four months—whatever cadence makes the most sense for you and your colleagues.

The work of narrowing down content standards can feel daunting. Priority standards are not always obvious, otherwise this wouldn't be the point of debate in education that it is. But know that creating a list of priorities is an effort well worth your time. It is work that will allow you to teach the most important content in greater depth and preserve time for students to actively transfer new and priority information from their short-term memories to their long-term memories. As we'll see in the next chapter, students must be given the space and time to grapple with new content in order to retain and truly learn it, and this work must happen soon after they've been exposed to new content. Attempting to teach too many standards reduces this activity time and, along with it, reduces learning.

Education consultant Larry Ainsworth, with whom I've worked, often says some standards are pillars of a fence, the rest are merely pickets. In teacher teams, you want to identify the pillars—the standards that without which, the entire fence would fall. These are the standards that your students must master by the end of the school year. This does not mean you will ignore all other standards altogether. It simply means that the focus skills of those deemed priorities are the skills you and your colleagues agree kids *will* attain by the end of the school year. From there, select non-priority standards can be the "pickets" of the fence and used to augment students' comprehension of and proficiency with priority standards.

Depending on the cadence you and your teacher teams choose to meet, you can identify priority standards in the appropriate batches to arrive at a list of fifteen to twenty standards that will be the focus of your school year. As you discuss

> Our mandate as teachers is not to cover; it's to help kids *discover.*

with your teams, always bear this in mind: Our mandate as teachers is not to cover; it's to help kids *discover.* Specifically, we didn't go into teaching to cover content. We chose this profession to help students discover knowledge, the depths of their cognitive power, and their unlimited potential. Let this greater purpose serve as the backdrop to your conversations with your teams. From there, questions to guide your thinking follow.

Questions to identify priority standards:

+ What are the skills students absolutely must have and be able to take action with once the school year is over? What knowledge and critical thinking skills must they be able to demonstrate? Which skills will ensure they advance to the next grade prepared to handle its content, work, and learning? Note: It's critical to answer these questions in the summer, as it will inform content priorities throughout the school year.

- Which standards most directly support the building of skills, including critical thinking, we've deemed most essential? Which standards appear to be less related to these skills?
- Which standards build upon other standards? Which can stand alone? Answering these questions will help ensure you avoid prioritizing a standard without also including those that must precede it to scaffold student learning. Or it will help pinpoint any standards that feel tangential to larger and core themes that will infuse your instruction for the year and can therefore be deprioritized.
- Which standards or skills appear across multiple grade levels and content areas? If some version of a standard appears across content areas, it likely means the skill is both difficult to acquire and foundational for the development of a variety of other skills and should therefore be prioritized.

Prioritizing Content for Your Lesson

Merely creating a list of prioritized standards will alleviate an enormous burden when it comes to prioritizing content for individual classes. In a way, the process of deprioritizing certain standards mirrors our brains' pruning process, or forgetting, of less critical information. With a much more manageable list of standards in front of you, your mind will feel less cluttered, overwhelmed, and stressed. You will be able to approach priority standards with greater cognitive energy and focus, which will allow the priority points within a standard to bubble up much more readily. Priority points get even more helpful from there. They don't just inform your lesson (or multiple lessons to cover a broader priority standard); they also inform the *Activity* and *Summation ATLAS* components. Prioritization of content allows you to design instruction and learning with greater clarity, focus, and efficiency.

In every class, you'll need to allot time for the activity, which we'll dive into in the next chapter. Prioritized information prepares students to take action with that information, and it's in the action that kids begin to understand and build memory of content. As you plan your lesson, factor in time for an activity, which is the main event of learning. From there, you can back into how much time you will devote to the *Lesson* component, or the knowledge transfer to students.

> Prioritization of content allows you to design instruction and learning with greater clarity, focus, and efficiency.

Use the following questions to help you prioritize the content within a standard and in advance of every lesson.

Questions to identify priority information for a lesson:

- At the end of this lesson or unit, what are the skills my students must have? What content or concepts must they remember? Answering these questions first is foundational. The answers will inform the most important points and takeaways of each lesson (as well as the activity and summation parts of class).

- How much time do I need to adequately teach to these standards? What space exists in my week or month to allow me to revisit these standards with struggling learners?

- What supporting standards stem from and feed into the priority standards? Which are necessary to scaffolding priority points? Which might not be? Which might actually be extraneous or unnecessarily confusing to students? In answering these questions, you will be able to present information hierarchically and also identify which points will require less time and reiteration.

If helpful, rank order points and double check the logical flow of how you've placed them in hierarchy.

+ What enrichment opportunities exist in and among non-priority standards to support continued growth for students who are proficient or advanced?

Designing Lessons for Student Retention: Best Practices

Just like the parishioners in Father Matt's church services, your students' attention is going to fade in and out throughout your lesson. Your students will also, of course, forget much of what you teach them. To circumvent these realities and to do your best to maintain students' engagement and promote their memories of what you want them to recall, follow the best practices of the *ATLAS Lesson* component.

First, the most likely lesson delivery mechanisms are lecture, video/audio/podcast clip, and close read. If you have other clever ways to transfer knowledge to students, by all means, include those as well. What matters is that, regardless of its delivery mechanism, you anchor the content around a handful of priority skills. The goal is to scaffold your students' comprehension by surrounding priority points with the most important supporting information and activities in the most logical way. You will use mnemonic devices, like repetition or imagery, to drive home priority points at least a few times in the lesson. This approach stands whether you transfer knowledge through lecture, video/audio clips, a close read, or some combination of each.

Structuring and delivering lesson design for retention and engagement:

+ Use your wisdom and judgment to determine how information needs to be ordered to scaffold student thinking and understanding and to make priority points obvious. Give more time, energy, and emphasis to the most relevant topics, skills, and key points.

- Reiterate priority points throughout the lesson. Use mnemonic devices and repetition to emphasize and indicate their importance. Rotate knowledge delivery modalities (lecture, video/audio/podcast clips, and/or close read) when doing so can draw greater attention to key points. In addition to promoting memory, diversification of instructional devices and tactics will function as mini attention getters to re-engage students whose attention spans may have lapsed. Devices and tactics include:
  - Repetition of key words or phrases that directly relate to and reiterate priority points
  - Questions that prompt students to think about priority points and keep them at the forefront of their brains
  - Match images to priority points to create picturing opportunities that support comprehension and recall
  - Leverage total physical response, hand gestures, or body movements associated with key points
- Pepper your lesson with quick exercises designed to check student engagement levels and to assess if students are latching onto priority points. Examples of such formative assessments include: quick write, think-pair-share, turn and talk, and self-assessment exercises. See chapter 6 for additional detail on these tools. While these are technically mini activities, they will provide insight as to how effectively you are structuring your lessons for retention and engagement.
- Be patient with yourself. Mastering lesson design optimized for engagement and retention will likely take some trial and error. Formative assessment data will clue you into where you might need a little more practice or intention in presenting information with hierarchy, or if you need practice identifying priority points or creating the most logical flow of the lesson with priority

points sufficiently emphasized. What matters most is that you remain courageously committed to gathering feedback from students as to their retention of what you want them to remember and making adjustments to your lessons as needed.

Additional best practices and key points of the Lesson component:

+ The forgetting curve means that you are accountable to your students to help them remember what you want them to know and be able to do. And forgetting begins the moment learning starts. This is an inescapable fact and one we can accept. Trust that, in using *ATLAS*, you are working around the fallible, forgetful brain and angling for your students' attention and retention anyway.

+ At the beginning of the school year—or this upcoming week, if you are in the midst of a school year—tell your students about the forgetting curve. Why not? This is empowering information for you and them. You can liberate them from beating themselves up for the natural process of forgetting. And you and your students can get on the same team of working to remember priority points. Let them know that you have their memories in mind and that you will do your best to help them identify the most important information they must retain in order to meet your high expectations and excel in your class.

+ While mild moments of stress can assist memory and learning, excess and prolonged stress impair both.[6] Use formative assessments often to identify when students are struggling unproductively as early as possible. Use scaffolding to ensure they struggle productively and persevere through confusion and into understanding.

+ Some students are visual learners, others are aural. To target the variety of learning styles in your classroom, rotate all information delivery devices as much as possible, including within a lesson. If possible, in addition to your lecture, weave in video and audio clips or a close read.

Long Live the Lecture

On that topic, let's talk lectures. Lecture has become a dirty word in education. So much so that some educational leaders are actively working to coach lectures out of classrooms. This is a fool's errand. We're never going to coach lecture out of the classroom. The fact of the matter is, lecture is one of the most logical and reasonable ways to transfer knowledge to students.

Lectures get a bad rap, sometimes justifiably so. For starters, relying solely on lecture for all learning will inevitably bore your students into oblivion. As we'll see in the next chapter, lecture alone also doesn't lend itself to deep learning. Furthermore, very few people are capable of lecturing effectively for a full forty minutes and maintaining the audience's attention the entire time. Because most humans cannot do this, lectures often get written off entirely as out of reach for most people and a guarantee of audience boredom. This is a baby-out-with-the-bathwater attitude, and one that I think misses a far more important point.

Students get bored and disengaged when learning is not made relevant to them, when they are not challenged, when they are not supported through productive struggle, and when they are deprived of opportunities to engage in activities to work with new content. This is a fact no matter how information is transferred to students. Lectures

> Lectures don't disengage students, at least not on their own. Uninteresting, low-rigor, and irrelevant instruction and learning disengages students.

don't disengage students, at least not on their own. Uninteresting, low-rigor, and irrelevant instruction and learning disengages students.

For many teachers, lecture is the simplest way to transfer knowledge to students. I, for one, am not going to lecture you to stop lecturing. My aim is not to make your job harder; it's to make it easier by encouraging you to play to your strengths. And certainly not by taking away the instructional approaches that allow you to teach most effectively and feel comfortable while doing so.

When it comes to lectures, what matters most is that they exist within the larger context of carefully orchestrated instruction and learning design that mitigates the risk of boring, disengaging lectures. *ATLAS* is such a design. When plugged into *ATLAS*, lectures will not be boring. Nor will they take up the entire class period. They will take only as much time as needed to emphasize priority points that students can then work with in the *Activity* component of *ATLAS*. They will be intentionally outlined and structured for optimal retention. You will lecture in a way that doesn't overwhelm your students with too much information, but rather feeds them the most critical points so that they know on which ideas to focus their thinking. Lectures will also be peppered with mnemonic devices that grab student attention when their attention naturally lapses. And they will include frequent formative assessments to break up the lecture and make sure students remain on track.

ATLAS is where boring lectures go to die and engaging lectures come to life. Lecture all you want. Just do it with thought, intention, and care.

CHAPTER 6

Activity

In 2019, scientists from Harvard published findings from an experiment about hands-on learning vs. lecture learning for college students in an introductory physics course. Eight years earlier, the study's lead author, Louis Deslauriers, had released a study revealing that science students learn more from active learning, in addition to lecture, than from listening to lectures alone.[1] Despite this fact, Harvard students told administrators they felt they learned more from lectures and preferred them to hands-on learning opportunities. With evidence to the contrary in hand, Deslauriers was confused. He was determined to get to the bottom of this paradox and, hopefully, encourage more science students to ask for more hands-on learning classes.

Deslauriers and his team designed an experiment to measure both students' perceptions of how much they felt they learned and how much they actually learned after lecture classes and hands-on learning classes. All students in the study received eleven weeks of lecture. In the twelfth week, the students were divided into two groups. For the week's first class session, one group continued to receive only lecture by way of a "superstar" lecturer. The other half engaged only in hands-on learning. For the next class session, the groups swapped so that all students were given the opportunity to engage in active learning. After each class session, students were quizzed on what they learned and filled out a survey on their perceptions of the class and their learning.

What Deslauriers and team discovered was both elucidating and fascinating. Students reported that they felt like they learned more from the lecture. Yet, their test scores proved otherwise. Students who had just engaged in hands-on learning tested better than their peers who had only listened to lecture.[2]

In an article in the *Harvard Gazette*, Deslauriers summed up the conclusions of the study: "Deep learning is hard work. The effort involved in active learning can be misinterpreted as a sign of poor learning. On the other hand, a superstar lecturer can explain things in such a way as to make students feel like they are learning more than they actually are."[3]

When I read Deslauriers's take on his research, I immediately thought of athletic coaching. For years, I've coached high school football. The specifics of coaching any sport vary, but athletic coaching methodology is almost always the same no matter the sport. At practice, coaches will explain a skill or a play. They will do this by the classroom equivalent of lecture. Often, coaches will weave in video footage to show a skill or play in action. Such teaching of skills is necessary, yet it is passive for the players. All they can do as they listen is imagine what it would feel like to put the skill—say, spiraling a football—into practice. After the explanation, athletic coaches always put their players on the field (or court) to do reps and drills to practice the skill or play.

When young football players first learn to throw a football, they mess up hundreds of times. Mastering that balance between spiral and force can be a challenge. Coaches will observe players' form and explain the adjustments they need to make in order to improve. Over and over again, players will throw. Coaches will watch and give feedback. Players will throw again, and the cycle repeats. This work feels hard to players, much harder than it felt to listen as coaches explain the skill and imagine themselves doing it. The road to mastering athletic skills is paved with countless upsets and frustrations. Players make mistakes. They feel they're not getting it or lack the capacity to master the skill. They get discouraged. But coaches tell them to stay the course. Because coaches know that the process works. No matter how hard practice may feel to players, they are on the proven path to improvement. With enough active practice, players will begin to see their own progress, overcome discouragement, and gain confidence in their skill.

Listening to the coach explain a skill is easy. It's easy to follow along with the coach's points and think you're grasping the concept. But practice inevitably opens players up to frustration and failure. It forces them to reconsider how they'd originally perceived the skill, which, through active practice, they are coming to understand with more clarity and depth. This is hard work. Work that, especially in those discouraging moments, can make players feel like they're not learning or growing.

Except they are. Listening is important. Listening is an essential ingredient of learning. But listening is easy. Action is hard. Action enables skill development that listening never could. Actively practicing skills is the only way kids can learn, grow, and work towards grasping ideas within a larger context and applying knowledge to various real-world circumstances. And what is learning if not directed towards these outcomes, the outcomes that enable our students to gain valuable critical thinking and career skills so that they may succeed, thrive, and self-sustain in their worlds?

> Listening is an essential ingredient of learning. But listening is easy. Action is hard. Action enables skill development that listening never could.

How Active Learning Promotes Deep Learning, Usable Knowledge, and Memory

The Teacher and the book are no longer the only instructors; the hands, the eyes, the ears, in fact the whole body, become sources of information, while teacher and textbook become respectively the starter and the tester. No book or map is a substitute for personal experience; they cannot take the place of the actual journey.[4]

So wrote John Dewey and his daughter, Evelyn Dewey, in their 1915 book *Schools of To-Morrow*. (No, that hyphen in their old-timey spelling of "tomorrow" is not a mistake!) John Dewey was among the most renowned education reformers of the turn of the century. Evelyn followed in his footsteps, devoting her life to increasing access to high-quality education for all, among other causes. They are both credited with reshaping how educators perceive their roles in instruction and student learning to this day.

In 1914, Evelyn and her parents visited Montessori schools in Europe. Inspired by the unique approach to learning they saw, Evelyn and John would go on to visit experimental schools across the United States. As they explain in their book, they were struck by the prevalence of "learning by doing" in these schools. In fact, *Schools of To-Morrow* holds the first known reference to this then-new term, "learning by doing." The Deweys saw that this kind of doing yielded far deeper learning for students compared to merely listening. It was through "doing," they observed, that students were able to embark on a journey of learning, where they were the active agents grappling with content rather than passive recipients of information.

Today, we call "learning by doing" active learning. While different people have different definitions, or even terminology, for this concept, the common thread is that active learning requires that students are 1) doing things and 2) thinking about what they're doing.

As the Deweys point out, the teacher and the textbook play supportive roles in active learning. It is a student process, not a teacher's process. In *How People Learn: Brain, Mind, Experience, and School*, a team of education researchers and experts contribute perspectives to create a composite for how students learn and how educators can create learning experiences accordingly. Ultimately, they are all advocates of student empowerment. In the introduction, editor John D. Bransford frames active learning as a mechanism to put students in charge of their learning.[5] It is through this kind of agency and ownership, he says, that students can construct facts into usable knowledge they can then apply to various circumstances and domains. By definition, any instance in which teachers do not give students opportunities to engage in a learning activity is not active learning. Such approaches would stop short of sending players onto the field to practice and refine the new skill their coach explained to them. It would leave them with only hearing about a skill, not practicing and obtaining it.

Yet as Bransford explains, activity alone can also fall short of true active learning. The quality of the activity matters. Action with information can produce its intended result—of enabling future application of new knowledge schema—only through activity that relies on metacognition. While not all learning activities are metacognitive, all metacognitive activities qualify as active learning. It's through metacognition that active learning derives its transformative power—the power to unlock student's capacity to "transfer their learning to new settings and events."[6]

Bransford frames metacognition as referring to "people's abilities to predict their performances on various tasks...and to monitor their current levels of mastery and understanding."[7] Instructional strategies that promote metacognitive active learning are those that "focus on sense-making, self-assessment, and reflection on what worked and what needs improving."[8]

When experts are working in the area of their expertise, they are using metacognition without their conscious awareness. It's a reflex, a habit. Bransford references research where area experts were asked to verbalize their learning as they wrestled with new information or attempted to solve a problem. As they worked, the experts simultaneously examined their learning, noting when they confronted new information and explaining the process they took to reconcile it with their preexisting understanding. Or they assessed when they'd hit a knowledge limit and needed to gather additional information to aid in deeper comprehension. In other words, metacognition was essential to their ability to assimilate new information in order to "adapt," or evolve and expand, their expertise.

Children can be taught these same metacognitive strategies that enable their growth and open up the potential for future expertise. Bransford mentions research showing that active learning can help students develop metacognitive strategies such as "the ability to predict outcomes, explain to oneself in order to improve understanding, note failures to comprehend, activate background knowledge, plan ahead, and apportion time and memory."[9] These and related strategies are accessible through learning activities that require students to do and to think about what they are doing in order to successfully complete a task. These tasks can be literally "hands-on," such as a science experiment. But they need not be. They simply must require action and metacognition.

Metacognitive activities are inherently engaging. They are, by definition, an active process. They do not allow students to sit quietly and absorb information or even just memorize facts. Metacognitive activities force students to consider information within the context of what they already know so that they can create new schema. That is, they must weave together facts—some previously understood, some new—to build a new mental construct. It is in this process of new schematic creation that information moves from the short-term memory to the long-term memory. Once information is in students' long-term memory, they can retrieve it in the future—either for summative assessment or when they confront new information that relates in some way and requires a preexisting schema to establish comprehension. They can transfer their learning to new settings and events, which is the promise of intentional active learning.

At the expert level, metacognition is usually an internal process, either as an internal monologue or a process that has become so automatic, no internal monologue is needed. As teachers, we can never assume students are learning metacognitively. It's up to us to design activities that require students to take action and think about the action they are taking as they progress. And it's up to us to build in opportunities for assessment that will allow us to gain insight into their internal learning monologues to detect the depth and consistency of their metacognition. When activity exists within the ATLAS methodology, you can rest assured that you have thoroughly laid the foundation to optimize active learning's outcomes.

> It's up to us to design activities that require students to take action and think about the action they are taking as they progress.

Activity the *ATLAS* Way

In *How People Learn*, Bransford summarizes the three cornerstones that shape how students learn as follows:

1. "Students come to the classroom with preconceptions about how the world works. If their initial understanding is not engaged, they may fail to grasp the new concepts and information that are taught, or they may learn them for the purposes of a test but revert to their preconceptions outside of the classroom."[10]

2. "To develop competence in any area of inquiry, students must: (a) have a deep foundation of factual knowledge, (b) understand facts and ideas in the context of the conceptual framework, and (c) organize knowledge in ways that facilitate retrieval and application."[11]

3. "A 'metacognitive' approach to instruction can help students learn to take control of their own learning by defining learning goals and monitoring their progress in achieving them."[12]

Through the *Attention* and *Transition* components of *ATLAS*, we are appealing to and leveraging students' preexisting knowledge as a bridge to new information and concepts. In the *Lesson* component, we are laying the foundation of factual knowledge. By prioritizing new information and facts and presenting them hierarchically, we are reducing "noise," or less critical information for students. We are guiding them to coalesce key ideas into conceptual understanding such that they can begin to take action with this information.

In the *Activity* component, we are reinforcing the second cornerstone of learning and addressing the third. Through an intentionally metacognitive activity, students are able to wrestle with the content they just absorbed in the lesson. Action with information allows students to create a conceptual framework that contextualizes new information. It gives them the opportunity to organize knowledge into an entirely new schema, which creates the potential for it to be retrieved and applied to other circumstances in the future. Activity also ensures that we hand over the work of learning to the students, supporting them as needed but holding them accountable as the primary players in their learning journey.

Let's think about how students learn in terms of our definition of student engagement. The *Attention*, *Transition*, and *Lesson* components stoke student *curiosity*. The metacognitive *Activity* is where we empower them to *participate* in active learning and *persevere* through the inherent and inevitable challenges and setbacks students confront when they are asked to apply skills to new circumstances. *ATLAS* aligns with how students learn. It engages their whole selves in a learning process that deepens their understanding and promotes retention of new concepts for future application.

What we must remember, though, is that instruction that stops short of a metacognitive activity stops short of learning. No athletic coach would ever stop practice at the end of the explanation and video components of the practice. Nor would a coach ever say "Now that we've discussed how to spiral a football, tomorrow we'll discuss how to kick one. Have a great evening." Or "My explanation of throwing ran long. We're out of time to get on the field and practice. Please practice at home, and we'll discuss kicking tomorrow." Engaging in activity with the skill or play is the main event of all sports coaching and all player learning and growth.

The same is true of academic learning and growth. Yet we often forget this. It can be perfectly acceptable, or at least common, to transfer knowledge to kids and consider the learning done. With sports, laying information at kids' feet and never giving them the chance to take action with it means they'll never develop the technical skills necessary to compete and win. In school, this means students will never develop the skills and depth of understanding necessary to apply information, nor will that information stand a chance of lasting in the long-term memory.

In the *Lesson* component, you put effort—big effort, starting in the summer with narrowing down all standards to fifteen to twenty priority ones—into focusing on priority information optimized for student retention. *Activity* the *ATLAS* way is where you ensure your efforts up to this point don't go to waste. And it's where you ensure your students' potential to remain engaged in their learning and to learn deeply are not lost.

When you transfer information to students—be it through lecture, video and audio clips, close reads, or some mix thereof—you are funneling it into their short-term memories. The forgetting curve tells us that if students do nothing to promote retention of that information as soon as possible, it'll be gone from their memories within a matter of hours. *Activity* is the only way students can begin to turn facts into usable knowledge, stored in the long-term memory for future application.

Active Learning for K-12 Learners, Across Subject Areas

Several studies have shown active learning's incredible impact on learning outcomes. As one example, a team of biologists from University of Washington, Seattle and University of Maine, Orono conducted a meta-analysis of 225 studies that compared test scores and failure rates of students who received only lecture and students who received at least some hands-on learning in addition to lecture. They found that students who received only lecture were 1.5 times more likely to fail a course than peers whose courses included some hands-on learning.[13] Another study out of the University of Chicago used fMRI brain scans and discovered that when students spoke about their involvement in a hands-on learning activity, sensory- and motor-related parts of the brain were activated.[14] Activation in these areas of the brain, which came by way of a physical experience with content, is associated with better class and test performance. Researchers noted these benefits remained intact weeks later.

These findings are consistent with a series of similar research studies on the many ways hands-on learning boosts learner outcomes.[15] The problem with these studies? They are all done with college students in STEM classes. Science experiments lend themselves to straightforward active learning research because such tasks are so blatantly hands-on. But for those of us who teach kindergarten, fourth-grade math, freshman social studies, or any K-12 class—what, if anything, can we draw from active learning research done in college STEM classes?

This is the precise question Garvin Brod set out to answer through an inspection of available research for his 2021 paper "How Can We Make Active Learning Work in K–12 Education? Considering Prerequisites for a Successful Construction of Understanding." Brod, a professor at Leibniz Institute for Research and Information in Education in Germany, notes that one of the reasons studying active learning in K-12 settings is so difficult is because terminology of the concept is so inconsistent. Nonetheless, in teasing out active learning from numerous studies, he is optimistic about active learning's potential to drive better learning outcomes for K-12 students.

Here's the thing: Undergraduate students derive greater benefits from active learning than do younger students. Just as adult experts derive even more benefit from it than do college students. This should not surprise us because active learning requires metacognition, and metacognition is a skill that improves when used again and again, over time, and in a range of settings. Active learning is also, as Brod points out, a function of preexisting knowledge.[16] Of course active learning will be of even greater benefit to those who have more preexisting knowledge.

If a person is a lifelong learner, then the benefit they will derive from active learning should grow exponentially throughout their life. Active learning across a life enables one to develop an expertise that makes them valuable in the workforce. Within this view, our job as K-12 educators is to get young children started on this journey in all subject areas. It's to provide for them metacognitive activities that

> Active learning across a life enables one to develop an expertise that makes them valuable in the workforce. Within this view, our job as K-12 educators is to get young children started on this journey in all subject areas.

will allow them to, bit-by-bit, learn more about how they learn. To practice putting information to work. To gain more context and usable knowledge. And to learn how to apply their expanding usable knowledge to increasingly diverse settings and events.

When it comes to a lifetime of gathering the fruits of active learning's labor, the work has to start somewhere. Students are far better off and their futures are far brighter if that work starts with us, K-12 educators.

To that end, Bord points out that K-12 students require scaffolding and support in active learning. Just how supportive and hand-holding we are as K-12 educators is a function of our students' age, experience with active learning, background knowledge, and metacognitive skills. Don't be afraid to scaffold like crazy as your kids engage in intentional activities, especially if they are younger and especially if they are newer to relying on metacognition for active learning. They are not college students, and we cannot expect them to engage in hands-on learning with hands-off teacher support. Bord notes that if we fail to provide sufficient support, then active learning can do more harm than good. But this is by no means a reason to shy from it in your classroom. That, too, will do more harm than good. Bord suggests that, as needed when overseeing active learning, we offer support like prompting students to perform a specific action, providing them with some piece of the action or solution, or teaching them useful strategies they can apply to the task.[17] The challenge, Bord points out, is knowing just how much guidance to provide. Too little and too much can reduce the benefit of active learning.

The importance of scaffolding our students through metacognitive activity is why carving out time for it in our classes is so important. What we know about the need for metacognitive scaffolding is an argument against leaving students to practice spiraling the ball at home, so to speak. If we relegate active learning to homework alone, we won't be by students' side to scaffold them through the metacognitive aspects.

This is ripe for a scenario where the metacognitive work could do more harm than good. When it comes to metacognitive active learning, do some first in the classroom and use homework only for reinforcement.

Witnessing your students engage in metacognitive activities is also the only way you can develop an intuition for the right balance of support and scaffolding—and you absolutely will develop this intuition. It will require some trial and error. It will require routine formative assessments with your students to gauge their success in obtaining metacognitive strategies and applying them. It will require that you also assess yourself or engage trusted colleagues to assess you. To this end, I strongly encourage you to work on this skill with professional learning teams. Support each other and stay the course. Because your effort is the equivalent of making sure that, every day, your students get out on the field and you can observe their form as they throw the ball. This is the only way your students will excel in school and grow into lifelong learners.

Active Learning's Additional Benefits

In case the scant research on active learning across subject areas at the K-12 level has left you still somewhat doubtful of its power and relevance for us, let's look at all the ways active learning links to what we do know elicits deeper learning and to what we value in education. When an activity demands that students analyze and assess their learning as they do work, active learning is cognitively, socially, and emotionally engaging work that reaches more students. Here's how:

- ✦ Active learning requires higher-order cognitive skills: Listening involves the two simplest and lowest forms of thinking on Bloom's Taxonomy: remembering and understanding. Taking action with information while simultaneously thinking about our action requires the higher-order cognition skills listed in

Bloom's Taxonomy, which are, from least to most demanding: apply, analyze, evaluate, create.[18]

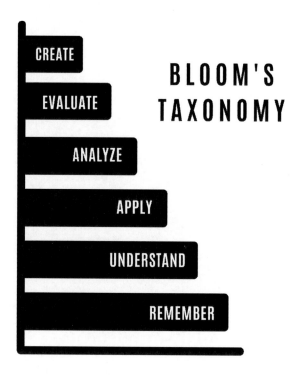

- Active learning is social-emotional learning: Metacognitive learning requires that students use a range of social-emotional skills, including self-awareness, self-management, self-assessment, personal responsibility and ownership, perseverance, persistence, problem solving, flexibility, determination, and more.
- Active learning is less susceptible to attention lapses. Recall from Chapter 3, students in a lecture class indicated attention lapses immediately and every few minutes. Importantly, these students were digesting information rather than applying it or taking action with it. Active learning demands greater student attention and focus. It mitigates against the consistency and frequency of attention lapses.

- Active learning is associated with "inclusive teaching."[19] In college-level STEM classes, research showed that active learning reduced the achievement gap for underrepresented minority and low-income students. While active learning boosted scores for all students, disadvantaged students gained disproportionated benefits. Unlike lecture, active learning ensures that every student is engaged, focused, and doing something. No student is allowed to fly under the radar or get away with not participating in and persevering through the learning.

Activities that Unlock the Benefits of Active Learning

When it comes to solid metacognitive learning activities that unleash active learning's benefits, options abound. In this section, I'll provide some of my favorites, but please know this is by no means a comprehensive list. Do your own research and create your own list. As you do, keep in mind the most important considerations and best practices of finding and using activities that deliver on the promise of active learning.

Important considerations and best practices of active learning strategies:

- Always strive to use strategies with an effect size of at least .4 or higher.
- The content of activities must always pertain to the lesson and give special attention to your priority points.
- Pin all activities to the same learning goal or goals for all students. Activities without goals that help students strengthen the skill you want them to develop or create the usable knowledge they need to obtain will fall short of the depth of learning students need and deserve.

- Weave quick formative assessments into the activity so that you can check that students are using metacognition successfully.

- Leverage technologies whenever possible that enhance your instruction and the quality of learning. Remember the first rule of *Bold School*: Avoid technology for technology's sake. Use tech only if you can confirm that it will bring substance to the learning activity, preserve opportunities for students to practice the skills and develop the knowledge they need, and provide students the opportunity to practice future-focused tech skills.

Concept Mapping

The first rule of concept maps is that they are not graphic organizers, and graphic organizers are not concept maps. Graphic organizers are black lines with white space, and kids respond to specific prompts to fill out the white space. Despite their name, graphic organizers do not require students to analyze, assess, and organize their thinking, as the "organizing" is done for them.

Concept maps, by contrast, are just blank space, and students are responsible for conceiving a means of depicting their thinking and understanding in a visualization. The ask of students is that they organize their thinking from larger to smaller concepts, which requires self-reflection and creativity. From there, they are free to create as it makes sense to them. Concept maps are a powerful way to fortify the connection between students' preexisting knowledge and new knowledge to build a new schema. They can be done the old school way, with pen on paper, or the bold school way, where technologies are intentionally leveraged to enhance learning and allow kids to practice relevant technology skills. Popplet, MindMup, and even Google Slides are excellent apps for concept mapping.

Choice Boards

Choice boards are a simple way to ensure students take ownership of their learning. Choice boards present students with some number of activity options, and students are free to select the activity they prefer based on what piques their interests. Choice boards enable voice and choice and allow students to regulate and pace their work. Their potential is further optimized when all learning activity options promote priority points and are tied to the same learning goal or goals, all activity options have some sort of metacognitive component, and there are activities that appeal to different learning styles, such as visual, auditory, kinesthetic, and tactile.

Jigsaw

Jigsaw is a collective learning activity in which students work in groups and are responsible for a certain chunk of content. In an ideal situation, groups include an even number of students, typically four to six students per group. Content is divided equally into as many chunks as there are students in a group. Individually, students review or read their content and list what they believe are the most important points from it in a jigsaw graphic organizer. Once this step is completed, students take turns teaching what they learned from their chunk of content to the group. As students learn, they list the additional important points from the group in their graphic organizer. Students also ask each other questions to gain clarity and understanding as needed.

Ultimately, students see a composite picture of the content. Teaching content to peers requires that students not only absorb information but also think about it, distill it, and clarify it for others. Once students have a complete and clear picture of the content, they can present what they learned or the conclusions they drew to the entire class.

Digital Breakouts

Digital breakouts are best—and easiest on the teacher—when done through apps like Breakout EDU or Google Forms. In digital breakouts, students work in teams to answer questions that the teacher has fed into the app. In answering all questions in one group correctly, students unlock the next group of questions. Questions should tie directly to the lesson content, and question groups should become increasingly more rigorous and relevant. Digital breakouts force students to remain more attentive during lesson segments of class when they are receiving information. They elicit the deepest learning when questions are essential and thought-provoking, as opposed to simple yes/no or single-word answer questions. While students can technically do digital breakouts individually, I generally advise against this. Individual breakouts too often lead to unproductive frustration. They also cause students to miss out on the metacognitive benefits of group work, which requires that students discuss and analyze their thinking and problem solving processes.

Modified Socratic Seminar

Before a Socratic seminar begins, participants must have engaged in a shared experience. For us, that is the lesson part of class, where all students received information transferred to them from you, a video, a podcast, or a close read. The seminar is then used to unpack, dissect, inspect, and apply new information to hypothetical scenarios. In a typical Socratic seminar, students are seated in two concentric circles, with a group of kids in the inner circle and a group of kids in an outer circle. The students in the inner circle are engaged in a conversation with the teacher and talking to each other. The kids in the outer circle are actively listening—or at least, that's the goal, but is it a reality? Probably not.

In a modified Socratic seminar, you keep the concentric circle approach—with one adjustment. Have all students in the inner circle face outward so that they are now seated in front of and looking at a classmate in the outer circle. Now all students are paired up and everyone is expected to engage in dialogue. When all kids are in position, give them a discussion prompt, which needs to be thought-provoking and demand higher-order thinking, not mere recall. The speaker will then speak on the topic for 45 seconds, after which the listener has 15 seconds to respond. After this, all kids in the outer circles stand up and move one chair to their right. For the next prompt, the students change roles so that the students who just spoke first are now the listeners and vice versa. (Note: If you have an uneven number of kids in your class, then there will always be a group with three students.) The success and substance of a modified Socratic seminar is a function of the quality of purposeful, provocative questions and pacing. Choose the pacing best for your students. Maybe for younger kids, the speaker will talk for twenty seconds and the listener will respond for ten seconds. No matter the time allotments, keep the exercise on time and moving.

Video/Infographic Curation

For this strategy, students can use a variety of technologies, such as WeVideo, Screencastify, iMovie, or ShowMe, to create a video or infographic that demands some kind of reflection on lesson content and application of new information. As teachers, it's our job to ensure that kids create these media for a reason beyond merely recalling points from the lesson or listing what they're thinking, and the purpose must tie to the same intended learning outcome for all students. Reasons can include summarization, reteaching, application of a new skill, asynchronous peer review, think alouds, or storytelling. Examples include: Asking kids to create a 90-second video identifying the steps and processes for solving math problems presented during a lesson. Or using iMovie to create a movie trailer highlighting the main idea and supporting details in a book they read.

Problem Solving Teaching

Problem solving teaching takes a specific approach to problem solving. Instead of listing the steps it takes to solve a problem, teachers emphasize what is needed in order to solve a problem and how one can find that information. Problem solving teaching is defined by five essential steps:

1) **Model**: Teachers model the act of solving a problem—not the solution. This starts with an essential question. As you work through the problem, explain your thinking, how you identify the resources and information you need to progress in solving the problem, and how you will go about finding these resources and information.

2) **Problem**: Next, present students with a problem to solve. It should be similar, but not identical, to the problem you solved, as you want the problem to enable productive struggle.

3) **Discuss**: Lead a class discussion about the essential questions and answers needed to solve the problem. Depending on your students, avoid spoon-feeding them the answers, but scaffold and guide their thinking as needed.

4) **Struggle**: Free students to solve the problem. Circulate the room to assess their work and thinking and identify students who may need individual support.

5) **Intervene**: While you might provide one-on-one support for individual students throughout the activity, also deliver three interventions to the entire class: an initial intervention to make sure students have started off on the right track; an intermediate intervention to scaffold for struggling students; a final,

summative intervention in the last minutes when, as a class, you discuss the problem-solving process. Note that in this final intervention, you are not giving kids the solution but using discussion to let them guide each other to it.

Problem solving teaching cannot work if you spoon-feed key resources, steps, or answers to students. To this end, this strategy is better reserved for when all students have mastered surface learning. Problem solving teaching yields deeper learning. When students are left to wrestle with the content, it's there that they can use those higher-order thinking and metacognitive strategies that make active learning so beneficial.

Peer Tutoring

You can think of peer tutoring as the umbrella category that includes peer teaching, peer review, and peer-to-peer metacognitive activities. No matter which specific version of peer tutoring you might use, two elements are important for all: One, peer tutoring should never be used to introduce new content. Two, it should be mutually beneficial to all students involved. In the absence of either of these requirements, peer tutoring can work against engagement, learning, and self-efficacy.

Activities to Gauge Students' Metacognition and Understanding

As we discussed, we cannot assume our students are using metacognitive skills. We must carve out time to confirm it. To that end, I suggest weaving into class lessons quick activities that require metacognition so that you can gain insights into how successfully and routinely your students are applying metacognitive skills.

Quick Write, Think-Pair-Share, Turn and Talk

These are straightforward metacognitive strategies that are easy to pepper throughout a class so that students can monitor their progress and you can gain insight into their metacognitive skills. In a quick write, students write for two minutes in response to a prompt. In think-pair-share and turn and talk, students turn to a classmate next to them to discuss a prompt for two minutes. You are free to come up with any prompts—so long as they require that students think about the learning. Two reliable prompts that use metacognition that I like are: 1) What reflection are you having based on your learning today? and 2) What's one area in your life you could apply new skills and knowledge learned today?

Self-Assessment

Metacognition is baked into self-assessment, which gives students the opportunity to assess where on a proficiency spectrum they see themselves today. For self-assessment to work, students need access to a relevant rubric and must understand the key benchmarks that indicate progress along the spectrum. Students must also not be left to self-assess in a vacuum. The success of this strategy rests on teacher involvement, particularly for students struggling to accurately place themselves on a spectrum. Teachers must help students recognize what kind of learning and practice they need in order to continue to improve along the spectrum. Students must also be given opportunities to apply refined understanding to another learning task and self-assess again to, ideally, see learning gains.

CHAPTER 7

Summation

It's time to wrap up *ATLAS*. So how about you write down one thing you've learned from each prior chapter of this book? Then, if you're so inclined, Tweet me your thoughts and reactions. Hopefully in writing down what you recall, you'll reinforce a few key points, and I'll also get a sense of what I might need to clarify going forward as I talk about *ATLAS* with audiences around the country.

Just kidding. That is not at all how I'm going to sum up *ATLAS* or this book. Doing so would be entirely forgettable and uninspiring. It would also emphasize my needs (what I can do better after it's way too late anyhow) over your needs (supporting the retention of what you've learned and leaving you feeling capable and empowered as you set off to put *ATLAS* into action). So devoid of emotional connection would an ending like this be that it might even change your perspective of all you've learned up to this point and leave you feeling far less enthused about using *ATLAS* at all.

How an experience comes to a close impacts how we feel about it and ourselves in relation to it. It also impacts what we will take from the experience and use from it going forward. I keep this fact in mind every time I drop off my kids at school in the morning. We have a ritual. Once I put the car in park, we all get out so that I can give both Charlotte and

Everett a great big hug. And then I look them each in the eye and say, "Work hard, be a leader, make good choices. I love you."

What I don't say is "Do you have your Chromebook? Your lunch? Did you remember all your home-work?" It's not that these things don't matter—they do and they are

> How an experience comes to a close impacts how we feel about it and ourselves in relation to it.

a reality of school. But I don't want to leave my kids' heads filled with my parental concerns as they set off to learn. I want them to remember what matters most—that I love them. I want them to *feel* something positive in their hearts that will carry them through their days. I want them to feel loved and confident so they are ready and energized to engage in their learning.

How we leave people matters. How we leave our *students* matters. How we use the last minutes of class to summarize what happened in it will inform how they feel about their time with us, themselves as learners, and the content they learned. It will also influence how they feel going into their next class or activity. As teachers, we have a choice as to how we use these final minutes. We can use them to simply rehash what was covered. We can do a summative assessment. We can leave students feeling failure, stress, or anxiety. Or we can leave them feeling like what they just learned mattered, that they're capable of applying new knowledge in a meaningful way, and that we believe they can suc-ceed and meet high expectations.

Hopefully the best choice is obvious. And achieving it is simply a matter of intentionally tying the priority points of the day to positive emotion.

Let's return to Miss Curry and her sixth-grade order of operations math class. After an engaging lesson and activity, there were only a few minutes left of class. So she asked students to stop working on the math problems and instead think about a typical experience they will encounter in the next few days where order matters. She then asked students to share their answers.

"When I eat a banana!" James—who'd declared in the beginning of class that he could eat the entire banana in nine seconds—shouted, to laughter from his classmates.

Another student yelled out, "When I give my baby sister a bath. I'll need to take off her clothes and diaper before putting her in the water."

"That's right!" Miss Curry said.

"Eat dinner then brush your teeth, not the other way around," volunteered a student.

"These are all really great examples, thank you," Miss Curry said. "Now what about how you all might order your homework tonight. Do you think you might do the most challenging homework first? Why?"

"Because it feels sooo good to get the hardest stuff out of the way, and then the rest feels easy," a student said.

"Exactly." Miss Curry said. "Did any of you have that experience today in class? Where PEMDAS initially felt really hard but got easier with practice? What did it feel like for PEMDAS to crystallize and begin to make sense?"

"Really satisfying," a student shared.

"It made me feel smart because I learned something new!" said another.

"That's right, when we push through what's hard to discover, we can understand challenging concepts; we gain confidence." Miss Curry said. "And we gain new skills! Important ones, too. Skills that will show up outside of class. Just like order of operations, which shows up in our lives constantly. And here's the thing, class—order of operations is here to help. PEMDAS tells you how to tackle math problems. But the concept of order of operations tells you how to think through a problem or a series of tasks so that you tackle them in the most efficient and logical way possible. It helps us avoid wasted time and a lot of frustration.

Order of operations is your friend! I encourage you to take it with you to help you figure out the best approach to any situation.

"It's also your ticket to more complicated math problems. So I want you all to be really proud of yourselves today—you learned a new tool and skill that is going to help you advance to more challenging math problems. Class, I want you all to know you are capable of learning how to solve more challenging math problems." Miss Curry said.

"This week, we'll continue using PEMDAS until we all have it down pat. Then, together, we'll begin even more exciting and tricky math problems—which I know you ALL are capable of handling. Great job today persevering through new and important information. See you tomorrow."

Masterfully and in a matter of minutes, Miss Curry recapped the significance of order or operations, explained to students what comes next, and reinforced her belief in their ability to do challenging things. But perhaps most importantly, she tied the lesson of the day to positive emotion to activate in her students a positive association between themselves, the content, and their capacity to learn.

Start to finish, Miss Curry taught like an *ATLAS* pro. She stoked her students' curiosity immediately at the start of class. She prioritized content as she lectured. Using problem solving teaching and guided practice, she navigated students through a series of problems, all the while checking for understanding and attention. When it was time for the activity, she asked each student to design a math problem that included parenthesis, exponents, multiplication, division, addition, and subtraction and whose answer revealed something about themselves. Examples included their age, the number of pizza slices they've eaten in a single sitting, and the number of siblings in their family. When it was time to sum up the class, she left them feeling joyful and excited to look for order of operations in the ordinary. In other words, she engaged her students even as they filed out of class, and she set them up to return to class the next day ready to engage in challenging, relevant learning all over again.

Emotion in Learning

Emotions are a fact and reality of instruction and learning because they are a fact and reality of being human. Emotions are happening in our schools and classrooms at every moment, whether we're aware of it or not. And they are inextricably linked to the impact of our instruction and the stickiness of the learning our students experience in our classrooms.

> Emotions are a fact and reality of instruction and learning because they are a fact and reality of being human.

Mary Helen Immordino-Yang, Professor of Education, Psychology, and Neuroscience at the University of Southern California, is renowned for her research on how emotion influences learning and the consequent implications for educators. In her 2015 book, *Emotions, Learning, and the Brain: Exploring the Educational Implications of Affective Neuroscience*, Immordino-Yang explains that neuroscientists used to believe cognitive and emotional processes were separate and had no influence on each other. Many even thought that emotions were a distraction from cognitive processes, such as learning and decision-making. In this paradigm, one's emotional state of the moment would have no effect or a negative effect on his or her decision-making and rationale.

However, in the late 1980s, research of people who'd suffered injury or stroke that impaired the emotional processing parts of their brains forced a shift in neuroscientific consensus. These patients began making unusual decisions that diverged from their pre-stroke or pre-injury behavior. Some made decisions that put their physical health or lives at risk. Others behaved in ways toward people that showed a complete lack of sympathy or empathy. Researchers noted that where these behaviors would have once elicited fear, regret, shame, or embarrassment from these patients, they felt no such emotions. They also failed to learn from their behaviors and make better decisions in the future. Researchers deduced that a lack of emotions did, in fact, have a huge impact on cognition and rationality. In the absence of emotional factors being incorporated into their cognition, these patients' choices were different and their judgments made irrational relative to their pre-injury or pre-stroke selves.[1] Interestingly, in a laboratory setting, the patients could articulate why their poor judgments or treatment of others was, intellectually speaking, misguided or wrong. Yet out in the real world, without the feelings of fallout from poor decisions, they lacked the ability to make better decisions. "These patients have lost their ability to analyze events for their emotional consequences and to tag memories of these events accordingly," Immordino-Yang writes. "Their emotions are disassociated from rational thought, resulting in compromised reason, decision making, and learning."[2]

With a healthy brain, a human has a subjective reactive feeling to an experience that informs their cognitive process in the moment. They are able to "tag" the emotion to the experience such that they can remember how the experience made them feel and apply this learning to a range of scenarios in the future. When we are driving on an interstate, we know that speeding—no matter how thrilling it may feel—can risk an accident that could harm us and others. Fear of such an outcome helps us keep to the speed limit, today and in the future. If we were to run into someone dressed in clothes we found unflattering, the anticipation of feeling regret or shame if we were to offend this person by sharing our opinion would tell our brains to keep our mouths shut and keep it polite (something I'm still learning as a husband). Our emotional reactions teach us how to perceive, think, and behave. As Immordino-Yang summarizes, emotions "are not add-ons that are distinct from [people's] cognitive skills. Instead, emotions, such as interest, anxiety, frustration, excitement, or a sense of awe in beholding beauty, become a dimension of the skill itself."[3]

That emotion is an inseparable dimension of cognition has huge implications for us as educators. First, it forever debunks the long-held notion that learning is purely cognitive and academic. Learning is just as much an emotional experience as it is an academic one. How our kids *feel* in our classrooms and schools has a material impact on the quality and durability of their learning. As Immordino-Yang writes, "It is literally neurobiologically impossible to build memories, engage complex thoughts, or make meaningful

> How our kids feel in our classrooms and schools has a material impact on the quality and durability of their learning.

decisions without emotion."[4] Specifically, a positive emotional state is linked to better learning outcomes, and a negative emotional state is linked to poor learning outcomes.[5] Whereas positive feelings can promote retention and recall, negative emotions can inhibit both.

Our students are constantly having subjective emotional reactions in our classrooms, and they are tagging these feelings to the experience of learning. In turn, this creates an emotional memory associated with the cognitive process they're using and the knowledge they're learning.[6] Put simply, they are going to remember their experience in our classrooms either positively or negatively, and this will directly impact if they retain what they learn and can apply it in the future. It is for this reason that I included "student disposition" in our definition of engagement. Emotion and engagement are inextricably linked. Student disposition as part of engagement's definition is both a reminder and a rally cry. It is true that we can impact our students' emotional state only so much, as it is a function of their natures and countless things happening outside of our classrooms. But it is a rally cry in that we must do everything we can to positively influence how our students feel when in our classrooms.

How do we do this? How do we imbue our classrooms with positivity such that it might break through our students' emotional states and increase the likelihood of deep and lasting learning that they can use in the future? We do this by removing as many barriers to positivity as possible and then closing class by explicitly tying learning to real-world relevant situations and to student self-efficacy. We do this through *ATLAS*.

How *ATLAS* Optimizes Positivity— Implicitly and then Explicitly

In Disney-Pixar's *Inside Out*, eleven-year-old Riley and her family move from their home in Minnesota to San Francisco. While the plot is rooted in Riley's difficult transition to a new hometown, most of the movie takes place in her brain. Riley's brain is run by her "emotion committee": Joy, Sadness, Anger, Fear, and Disgust, with each emotion personified by a different character. As Riley struggles to navigate life in a new city, at a new school, surrounded by new people, Sadness overwhelms her other emotions. The action of the movie revolves around the committee's attempts to get Joy back at the helm of the control panel. The takeaway is that, all things being equal, joy is our dominant and default emotion. When it's not calling the shots, something is off kilter that needs to be rebalanced.

For all its charms and cleverness in normalizing difficult emotions for kids, *Inside Out* didn't quite get human emotion right.[7] One's default emotional state is individual. One's emotional state at a given moment is also highly subject to change based on external stimuli or internal thoughts. In the average brain, various emotions are duking it out for the top spot in a given moment. Even various negative emotions will fight each other for the floor. But if there is one emotion with the competitive edge, it's fear. Because in healthy doses, fear is designed to keep us alive and safe. And, above all, we evolved to stay alive.

Immordino-Yang explains the evolutionary reason fear tends to drive the car for most of us.[8] Fear taught us which plants might be poisonous and therefore needed to be avoided. It taught us that fire can burn, tigers can prey, and dirty water can make us sick. The emotional reactions to these dangers augmented prehistoric humans' ability to learn and influenced their future decisions. Drawn out overtime, this emotional learning sustained human evolution and survival. Without fear, we would have died out as a species.

While modern threats are mostly different from those that evolved our emotional capacity, this capacity's essential job—to keep us safe from harm—remains intact. Recall the patients who'd suffered injury to the emotional processing parts of their brains—their inability to feel fear allowed their cognition to steer them right into life-threatening situations, like driving twice the speed limit on the highway or eating an exclusively unhealthy diet. Or it prompted them to insult others; in an evolutionary sense, this could have alienated prehistoric man from "the group" and decreased their odds of survival. In a modern sense, it's well known that emotionally and literally isolated individuals are more prone to disease and have a shorter life span.

At school, fear might keep students "safe" from failing grades or social isolation. In healthy doses, fear does this by compelling students to do their homework by deadline or to reach out to others to make friends, respectively. It can help students remember that the point of engaging and working hard in school is to prepare themselves for healthy, productive, self-sufficient futures. But just as with any so-called negative emotion, when fear runs amok or outlasts its purpose, it can create all kinds of issues for us.

If we think about school as a setting rife with countless stimuli competing for emotional reactions from our students, far too many stimuli are likely to evoke negative emotions, and far too often. Deadlines, tests, homework, grades, cliques, and social issues—each of these things is fodder for negative feelings. Layer on top of this alarmingly rising rates of depression and anxiety in today's children, and school can feel like anything but a safe, welcoming, positive place. In fact, for way too many students, it can feel like a serious pressure cooker or place of painful isolation.

When outside forces are not attempting to counterbalance our students' stresses and anxieties, then our students can get stuck in a downward spiral. Just as struggle can be productive when scaffolded and transitory, moments of stress can motivate students to apply themselves more or search for a different, more effective approach to a problem.[9] But when struggle or stress becomes chronic, it impairs the brain's capacity to process and retain information.[10] Without intervention, the more stressed one is about their school performance, the more their performance might suffer, the more stressed they will become, and so on in an escalating cycle. Eventually, such students become candidates for near total disengagement from school. Often, these are the apathetic students—the ones who seem never to care about their learning. But the odds are that they've been so defeated by disappointment in themselves or from feeling like a failure that they've just checked out. If one doesn't care, one can't get hurt. This, too, is a form of survival, a manifestation of too much fear.

If we accept that survivalist-driven fear is generally our students' default, then we can make decisions to ensure their fear remains in healthy balance. We can guide students to learn how to use it to their advantage. We can layer it with much more positive and affirming emotions to counterbalance it and create positive associations with learning, where fear motivates but does not dominate.

Immordino-Yang identifies a certain category of positive emotions as capable of counterbalancing fear and unleashing the deep learning that students can apply to various future circumstances. And this category includes emotions of depth—awe, wonder, curiosity, joy, interest, hope, sympathy, empathy, love, interest, surprise, to name some. These are not cheap emotions that we can win with cheap tricks. We can give our students candy 'til the cows come home, and all this will achieve is Pavlovian sugar craving when students walk into our classrooms. Even the carrot of good grades will fall short in eliciting the deeper positive response we want students to feel in our care. External and temporary rewards just won't cut it. We have to learn how to bring forth the deep emotional reactions, such as wonder and interest, that yield deep learning. This is hard work, as Immordino-Yang points out, but worth it because it is "essential for the development of truly useful, transferable, intrinsically motivated learning."[11]

Imbuing our classrooms with positivity is a function of both removing the triggers of too much or chronic negative emotion and explicitly linking learning to positive emotions. When it comes to achieving just the right amount of otherwise negative emotions, such as the mild doses of stress or frustration that can motivate productively, teachers must walk a fine line.

ATLAS is designed to keep you right at the edge of too much struggle and predominantly and sufficiently in the camp of positivity. *ATLAS* guides you to remove barriers to deep learning. With the *Attention* and *Transition* components, you are opening class using a topic with which students are already familiar. You are avoiding a cold open where students must attempt to grasp at something they don't understand or find interest in something they see as inherently disinteresting, thus leaving them confused and bored from the first moments of class to the last. Instead, you are starting from a schematic they already have and bridging it to a new one, thereby optimizing their capacity to take in and comprehend new information. In the *Lesson* component, you have taken care to deliver information optimized for clarity and retention. You are avoiding relaying information in a messy, incoherent, disorganized manner that would needlessly confuse and stress out your students. In the *Activity* component, you are requiring that your students use metacognition, which dramatically increases the likelihood that they will retain information and be able to apply it in the future. Meanwhile, frequent and quick formative assessments are baked in so that you can immediately intervene when students might be on the edge of too much confusion or unproductive struggle.

The *ATLA* components of *ATLAS* are your insurance policy against all those stressors just waiting to pounce on our students, invade your classrooms, and have a deleterious effect on learning. Instead, you are clearing the runway of excessive negativity and paving the way for positivity. When students are handed learning opportunities optimized for positivity, then they will be far more likely to naturally have positive reactions to it. When your students make the connection between an existing schema to a new one, they will move from curiosity to surprise. When they are following your hierarchically presented priority points, they will feel interest and confidence. When they engage in a hands-on, metacognitive learning activity that demands emotional processing in addition to cognition, they will feel a range of social emotions, such as tenacity, wonder, perseverance, a sense of discovery, and, ultimately, satisfaction and joy.

The feeling kids experience when they walk in the door can't be boredom, and the feeling they feel when they leave can't be failure. *ATLA* avoids boredom, ensures engagement, and implies positivity and a feeling of success from the start of class. The *Summation* component is where we bring in positivity explicitly. It's where we speak with intention and a plan to, literally, end class on a positive note.

How to End Class the *ATLAS* Way

Summation is simply what you say and what you ask of students in the final minutes of class. When done the *ATLAS* way, it protects you from squandering all your effort and all your students' learning up to the last few minutes of class. It ensures students leave your class just as engaged as they felt throughout it.

Summation must achieve three aims:

1) **We must reiterate the relevance of what students just learned to their lives inside and outside of our classrooms. In short, we have to answer for students: "What's in it for me?"**

   Given that emotions evolved to keep us alive and safe, we have emotional reactions to things that in some way feel important to our survival. To things that feel totally irrelevant to our survival—even if they are but we don't know it—we have a neutral or negative reaction. In a modern world, survival includes our capacity to thrive and gain and maintain self-sufficiency. Therefore, our emotion-cognition will naturally focus on those things that can support thriving and self-sufficiency. More simply, we pay attention to what matters to us and ignore what doesn't.

   When this comes to knowledge and skills, we are far more likely to pay attention to, work to learn, and put energy into retaining knowledge and skills we believe can enhance our ability to thrive in life. We will naturally ignore those that appear to have no relevance to our futures. As Immordino-Yang puts it, "the brain is highly metabolically expensive tissue, and evolution would not support wasting energy and oxygen thinking about things that don't matter to us."[12] This means that if we as teachers fail to explicitly link what we're asking students to learn to their ability to have successful careers and lives, then they will disregard what we teach them.

   ATLAS is designed to promote the real-world relevance of the content at hand throughout class. Yet it must be driven home one last time in the summation. It is, after all, through relevance that we connect emotionally to something. And it is through this emotional connection that we can learn to apply new information in the future to a range of circumstances.

2) **We must promote retention and our students' self-efficacy by linking learning explicitly to positive emotions. We must remember that students will be eager to discard memories and avoid future situations where they feel like failures.**

When learning is tagged to a positive emotion, what was learned is remembered with more clarity and accuracy and is more durable over time.[13] In the summation, we have an opportunity to drive home positive emotions to, one last time, do what we can to help our students retain what they learned in this class so they can apply it in the future.

We can also intentionally use and explain positive emotions in a way that simultaneously promotes students' self-efficacy. Self-efficacy is the belief that we can achieve difficult things and succeed in a given circumstance or domain. Chronic negative thoughts and low self-confidence or esteem inhibit or erode our self-efficacy. We *ATLAS* teachers are simply not going to let erosion of self-efficacy happen in our classes. Not on our watch.

The reality is that many of our students may not know that struggle and frustration can be productive or stress can be motivating. They may not know that just because something feels hard doesn't mean they're inherently incompetent or incapable. That struggle, stress, and confusion can be leveraged for gain is not exactly an intuitive concept—including to families and caretakers who might, unfortunately, reinforce a child's perception that they lack talent or aren't smart.

In an *ATLAS* classroom, however, all students are going to learn that they are inherently talented, gifted, capable, and brimming with potential. They're going to learn this because we're going to tell them—again and again, every day if we have to. We're going to teach and remind them that struggle, stress, and even failure are merely feedback, telling us that perhaps we need to try a different approach. *Summation* is an opportunity to drive these messages home, just like I do every day at drop off with my own kids at school. If it's important enough for my own children, then it's important enough for all children.

> In an *ATLAS* classroom, however, all students are going to learn that they are inherently talented, gifted, capable, and brimming with potential.

We can do this by articulating the emotional journey your class just experienced. In a way that is appropriate for the lesson and activity of the day, explicitly remind your students that they just learned something difficult. This means that they participated in a challenging activity, struggled productively, overcame setbacks, persevered to new understanding, and achieved deep learning, or are well on their way to doing so. Link their effort to the confidence they rightfully earned in class, or to validation in their capacity to grow by applying themselves and practicing a new skill. Turn the seemingly negative positive and the positive more positive.

3) **We must reveal what comes next.**

In your summation, briefly share what comes next in your students' learning. You don't need to go into a lot of detail here. The point is to manage expectations so that your students can mentally and emotionally prepare for the next class or next unit—whatever the "next" may be. This is an opportunity to seize the positivity of the moment to get your students feeling excited about what they've done and what's going to follow.

Additional Best Practices of Summation

+ Invite your students into your summation. Ask them how they see what was learned in class as relevant to other circumstances. Ask them how they struggled and overcame. Ask them if and when they felt wonder, curiosity, or delight as they learned. Ask them to name the positive feelings they felt in class. By including students in your summation, you will keep them actively engaged in class up to the last minutes of it. You will also unburden yourself of what can easily devolve into the same script delivered at the end of every class. Furthermore, the identification and naming of emotions is a social-emotional skill in and of itself that develops emotional intelligence and is worth asking students to practice.

+ Just as we are dealing with human, emotional students, we are human, emotional teachers. You're not going to be a ray of sunshine every day, and that is OK. Life happens, and some days we're just off. Or some days our students are just off. If you sense a collective negativity of any form in your class on a given day, don't beat yourself up. Where appropriate, see it as an opportunity to confront difficult emotions, moments, and days with courage. I'm not saying you need to reveal to your students what happened in your morning or what is going on in your life that has caused you to be in a less than perfect mood. I'm simply saying that it's OK to say things like, "Today's class was really hard. Let's discuss why." From there, you can open up a discussion with your class about the inevitable challenges that emerge when doing hard work and how we can grow from them. You can invite your students to identify and name their difficult feelings and ponder how they can use them in the future to make a different decision or choose a more effective path to problem solving. You can also model this process by sharing a time you made a mistake in teaching (even if on that very day!) and recognized you needed to learn and improve for your students. Leading your students in such a discussion helps recast what felt more negative than not in a positive light. It opens up the possibility that you can still end even an "off" class on a positive note.

✦ Remember: *Summation* isn't about you. Closing class with a formative assessment that provides information you can't act on for at least twenty-four hours—long after it will do any good anyhow—is about you. Closing class the *ATLAS* way is about your students and how you leave them feeling as they leave your class and go onto the next. OK, and it's a bit about you, as well. Because it will leave you feeling as confident as possible that you just lead your students in genuinely engaging learning.

Summing Up *ATLAS*

Now let's revisit how I originally summarized *ATLAS* at the start of this chapter. Let's try again. Let's do better.

Teachers, you play among the most critical roles in our country—or in whichever country you live, if different from mine. The single greatest gift we can give children in our schools is not more stuff, more assessments, more technology, or

> The single greatest gift we can give children in our schools is not more stuff, more assessments, more technology, or even more instructional time. It's you.

even more instructional time. It's you. And it's the best, most confident, most effective, and most engaging version of you.

But let's be honest, being at our best has felt brutally difficult lately. Teaching our children has gotten so insanely, maddeningly, disturbingly, and needlessly complicated. Various interests, competing priorities, and stretched thin or overly-prescribed budgets have wedged their way in between us and what we know is best for our students. Let's allow those forces to do what they must and will, and let us instead focus on what we can control.

You can control exactly what you say, how you deliver content, and what you ask your students to do with it, every day. You can do this work haphazardly, or you can do it intentionally. No more excuses. You now have the same resource every great songwriter, storyteller, Disney screenwriter, and stand-up comedian possesses: You have a formula. In *ATLAS*, you have an engagement formula that works. One that allows you to be hyper intentional in your classes to elicit the deepest learning from your students. And one that allows you to be creative and have a little fun along the way.

You now know that how your kids feel in the first minutes of your class impacts if they will participate in the learning of the day. You understand that if you stoke their curiosity with something familiar, you can capture their attention. Then you can intentionally leverage the familiar and transition your students to the new information that is to come. You appreciate that human brains are fallible and forgetful no matter what. But you also know that if you identify priority points and present them hierarchically and repeatedly, you will clarify what your students must retain and augment their comprehension. And you know that when you ask students to take hands-on, metacognitive action with new information, they will learn the content deeply and prepare themselves to apply it flexibly to several related and unrelated circumstances in the future.

In other words, you know how to engage your students in their learning.

I promise you—as you set out to practice *ATLAS*, if you experiment, refine your approach, and, most importantly, get creative and have some fun with it, you will see a change in your students' engagement levels. In time, you will see them walking into your classroom genuinely curious as to what interesting thing you will teach them that day. You will see them voluntarily and excitedly participate in their learning. And you will see them willingly and reflexively persevere when things get hard—because they will have learned that the payoff of a little struggle is worth it. They will grasp that resilience translates to deeper learning and deeper self-confidence.

Meanwhile, you too will experience a confidence boost. You too will feel more engaged in your profession and your day-to-day. You too will feel a greater sense of resilience when all of those outside forces try to jam their way into your classroom and between you and your students. Because this time, you will have a rebuttal: You will be a master of the *ATLAS* engagement model, with the improved student outcomes to prove it.

My friends, this is the promise of *ATLAS*. When it's in the hands of a confident teacher like you, *ATLAS* can make you better today than you were yesterday.

I truly cannot wait for the growth that awaits you. I cannot wait for you to be a teacher—*that* teacher!—whose students cannot wait to come into your class, roll up their sleeves, do hard work, and learn. I hope you'll let me know how it goes and what you learn—about teaching, about learning, and about your students. Most of all, I can't wait to hear just how much you learn about yourself and your power to be a creative and engaging teacher, every day.

Teachers, you've got this. As we navigate the path of engagement together, trust that I will continue to joyfully walk this path with you. I'm humbled by your efforts and grateful to share this profession with all of you.

CHAPTER 8

ATLAS Exemplars

What follows are examples of *ATLAS* in action that I've witnessed from masters of the model. Each of these exemplars created lively, joyful, and most importantly, engaging classes. That said, to help you imagine implementing *ATLAS*, I have written them as though you are the teacher in each exemplar.

Some things to keep in mind as you review the exemplars:

+ Six exemplars follow and were chosen to represent a range of grade levels and subject areas. Please do read them all, as opposed to jumping to those that are your subject or grade level. Each varies and showcases different *ATLAS* choices. There is something to be gleaned from each of them, no matter what and who you teach.
+ While I am listing all exemplars in the *ATLAS* order, know that the teachers who delivered these classes toggled between components—such as breaking up the lesson with chunks of activity, or returning to their transitional phrase that pays to reinforce points, or interspersing attention getters to recapture students' focus.

ATLAS

The Formula for Engagement that Leaves You in the Driver's Seat

ATTENTION

The intentional opener to class that stokes students' curiosity and compels them to participate in the learning to follow.

TRANSITION

The schematic bridge between something familiar in the Attention getter and the new content to come.

LESSON

The transference of hierarchically-presented priority points that support students' retention of the information.

ACTIVITY

The metacognitive action students take with new information to reinforce retention and catalyze deep learning and understanding.

SUMMATION

The intentional connection of priority points to positive emotion to boost student self-efficacy.

WESTON KIESCHNICK

- You will notice that the *Lesson* components in these exemplars are the lightest on content. This is because you will determine the most important priority points based on the specifics of the content, the needs of your students and classroom, and larger academic and school goals.
- Conversely, the scripts for various components are comprehensive. This is only in an effort to be as clarifying and instructive as possible. Write your own scripts. Choose your own angles. Bring your own personality and wit into them. Have fun with this.
- Let these exemplars inspire you as you craft your own *ATLAS* classes. I also encourage you to revisit the best practices of each component in their respective chapters as many times necessary for them to become habit.
- Refer to the ATLAS infographic above, summarizing each step in the planning process as you design your own ATLAS lessons and classrooms.

Exemplar 1

Subject: Art
Grade level: Middle school and high school
Topic: Introduction to the Impressionists
Standard: Perceive and analyze artistic works and styles

ATTENTION

<u>Attention getter</u>
Enrolling question

<u>How it works</u>
Put an image of a famous impressionist painting on the wall or screen. For our purposes, we'll use the painting that launched the impressionist

movement, Claude Monet's "Impression, Sunrise," in which he painted a harbor in Normandy, France, at sunrise.

To begin class, ask students to take a minute to look at the painting. Then ask them to make a prediction about what the artist might have been feeling when he painted this work. Note: In this example, we're using the "predict" aspect of the reciprocal teaching instructional strategy. We'll address its other aspects in the Lesson component. Pro tip: Hold off on sharing the artist's and painting's name and this point so that students can approach class with the most open mind possible.

Enrolling question: "This is a painting of a harbor of the artist's hometown at sunrise. Think about the kind of impression it leaves on you. *Based on how the painting makes you feel, can you predict what the artist might have been feeling when he painted this?*"

Solicit answers from the class. As needed, prompt them to consider the colors, the setting, the subject, the brushstrokes, the use of light, and so on.

As students share their thoughts, interject with purposeful repetition to signal that important information is coming. Examples include:

- "That's right. You get the impression that Monet might have been feeling calm."
- "Some of you are getting the impression that he felt a little sadness."
- "No right answers here, just feeling. Just an impression."

TRANSITION

<u>Bridge the known to unknown</u>
Bridging the human feeling as a response to a visual to the concept of impressionist art.

<u>Script, with phrase that pays in italics</u>
"You've all shared wonderful thoughts, thank you. What's interesting about this painting, as opposed to one of a soldier on a horse or a queen on her throne, is the impression it leaves on you. You don't just see, you feel. The style of this painting *leaves an impression*, doesn't it. It's a bit different. It doesn't tell you exactly what is going on. *It leaves an impression.*

Class, this painting is from Claude Monet, one of the first impressionist painters. What he and other impressionists did was use a new artistic style to invite the viewer into the works of art by *leaving an impression* on their feelings. So let's learn more about the impressionists and analyze what we see and what we feel when looking at examples of their art!"

LESSON

<u>Information delivery</u>
Lecture

<u>Priority points</u>
Recall that we're using the reciprocal teaching strategy. Use lecture to further *clarify* the most important points students must remember about impressionism. This could be:

- Up to this point, the only acceptable subjects of art were those that were considered noble—royalty, battles, religion, etc. The impressionists rejected this tradition and painted everyday scenes—people at a train station, people eating at a restaurant, a mother on a walk with her child, etc.

- The founders of the movement were considered rebels, and early critics were offended by their break from tradition. Today, impressionism is considered one of the most important art movements in history.

- Impressionists were criticized for what looked like an "unfinished" appearance to their art. But this was intentional, as they wanted to give an "impression" of a scene rather than a precise representation of it. In this, they left room for the viewer to bring their own experiences to it and feel something personal.

ACTIVITY

Metacognitive activities
Choice Boards and Turn and Talk, woven into the reciprocal teaching strategy.

Give student pairs the ability to choose between one of three activities or two of three activities, time permitting.

Activity option 1: Summarize
Post four images of paintings on a wall or screen. Include only one impressionist painting. The others should be from different artistic movements, such as romantic, baroque, expressionist, cubism, art deco, and so on. Instruct students to identify which painting is in the impressionist style and summarize why they think this is the case. Students will then do a turn-and-talk to explain their summaries to a partner. Ask select pairs to share their summaries to the class.

Activity option 2: Question and predict

Post images of three paintings from different impressionist artists. Aim for different scenes and subjects, for example: a cafe scene, a nature scene without people, a domestic scene. Ask each student to write down one question they would ask any one of the artists about the painting. They then do a turn-and-talk with a partner to share their questions and predict what they think the artist's answer would be and why. Ask select pairs to share their answers and thoughts to the class.

Activity option 3: Clarify and predict

Post an image of one impressionist painting and one painting from another artistic movement that came before the impressionists and is in obvious contrast to it; for example, a highly "finished" painting from the romantic period. Ask students to write down the differences in style they observe between the two, aiming for about five points of difference for each painting. Then they are to summarize why they think this particular impressionist painting leaves a personal impression on the viewer and why they think the other painting does not. Pairs then do a turn-and-talk to share their questions and predict what they think the artist's answer would be and why. Ask select pairs to share their thoughts to the class.

SUMMATION

Making it personal and positive

"As we discussed, the impressionists were mocked and dismissed by art critics in their day. These critics didn't believe that ordinary people and scenes were worth capturing in painting. Monet, Mary Cassatt, Edgar Degas, Renoir—all of these artists were tired of how art left out ordinary people. They were tired of art that did not feel relatable or relevant to them and their lives. So they decided to do something about it.

What they were doing was using art to elevate common people to a higher level of importance and respect. They also believed that the viewers of art should be allowed to feel something personal in response to it, rather than be bystanders to it.

This is art as power. This is art as change. These impressionists were trailblazers who permanently changed art and how it was considered. They did it peacefully and they did it effectively. And we see this kind of art around us all the time. What are other examples you all know of where art was used to make change?"

Invite kids to share answers.

"These are all great examples. In the next week, put more thought as to why you believe art can be such a powerful way to push for change. Next class, I'd like you all to come with an example of art that you found moving and that changed the way you felt about something. Or art that made you think about something you'd not considered before. Or see something in a new way. Come ready to show and share your answer."

Exemplar 2

Subject: Writing
Grade level: Middle school
Topic: Introducing the persuasive essay
Standard: Support claim(s) with logical reasoning and relevant evidence, using accurate, credible sources and demonstrating an understanding of the topic or text

ATTENTION

<u>Attention getter</u>
Story

<u>Story script</u>
"My family and I went to the beach over spring break. I had the super painful experience of stepping on a jellyfish. It was not at all what I was expecting during what was supposed to be a relaxing vacation. You know what the solution for tempering the pain of a jellyfish sting is, right?"

Among the guessed responses, a student will eventually yell, "Pee on it!"

"That's right, pee! A lifeguard rushed over to me to help. He made the point that, um, I needed to get some pee on the sting ASAP. I was not happy about the idea. But he said he's seen this work a dozen times. He explained that there's a chemical in pee that neutralizes the jellyfish sting. So guess what? He persuaded me. And I got to learn the hard way that peeing on a jellyfish sting works.

Would you believe me if I said that PEEing on any writing meant to be persuasive makes it better? Yep, you heard that right. PEE on your writing, make it better."

TRANSITION

<u>Bridge the known to unknown</u>
Bridge a jellyfish sting and, yes, pee—artfully told in a story that recapped a lifeguard's persuasive argument—to the persuasive writing concept, PEE: point, evidence, explanation.

<u>Script, with phrase that pays in italics</u>
"Class, PEE stands for point, evidence, and explanation. Point, evidence, explanation. PEE. And when we want to write an essay to persuade someone to believe or do something, we're going to *PEE on it to make it better*. That's right, we're going to *PEE on our writing to make it better*."

LESSON

<u>Information delivery</u>
Lecture

<u>Priority points</u>
Persuasive writing is only persuasive if it follows the PEE structure:
- ⁜ Point: Logical reasoning
- ⁜ Evidence: Relevant evidence supported by accurate, credible sources
- ⁜ Explanation: Demonstration of understanding of the topic or text

ACTIVITY

<u>Metacognitive activity</u>
Peer review

<u>How it works</u>
Provide students an example of a brief persuasive essay that you know is lacking in at least one of the PEE components and is therefore in need of improvement. You can share the same essay with all students or a few different essays amongst the students.

Ask each student to annotate the essay as they read with the following symbols:

- Circle points
- Underline evidence
- Star explanation

When done reading, if students don't see all three annotation symbols, they can identify which PEE components the essay is missing.

Then ask students—either individual or in groups—to re-write the essay to include the missing PEE component or components.

Finally, using a rubric, ask them to assess their writing. Have they covered all PEE topics? And how so? What can they do to improve?

Ask select or all students to share one thing they need to do to improve their persuasive writing skills, which they will go onto apply to a writing assignment.

SUMMATION

<u>Making it personal and positive</u>
"People who write for a living dedicate their entire lives to improving their craft. Writing is rarely finished. There's always room for improvement. I expect you saw ways you can improve your persuasive writing skills, and that is not only OK and very normal; it's also great! You cannot spot opportunities for improvement if you don't know what is needed for something to be done really well. And when it comes to persuasive writing, you all now know what needs to be done for it to be successful. And what is that?"

Kids yell, "PEE on it!"

"That's right, PEE on your writing! PEE on your writing to make it better. Awesome job today. I can't wait to read your persuasive writing assignments and discuss them in the next class. Just remember—PEE is a mnemonic tool, kids. We're not on the beach here, and there are no jellyfish!"

Exemplar 3

Subject: Social studies
Grade level: High school
Topic: Difficult public policy debates, with a focus on euthanasia
Standard: Construct claims and revise counter-claims expressing and justifying decisions on public policy issues.

ATTENTION

<u>Attention getter</u>
Video

<u>How it works</u>
Play the clip from *Da Ali G Show*, in which Sacha Baron Cohen's character confuses "euthanasia" with "youth in Asia." (Note: This clip is from season 3, episode 5 called "Jah." To find just this clip, search "Ali G medical ethics" on YouTube.)

TRANSITION

Bridge the known to unknown
Connect an actor and comedy show with which kids are familiar to the unfamiliar and serious topic, where humor is leveraged to put students somewhat at ease as they wade into a difficult debate.

Script, with phrase that pays in italics
"Euthanasia…funny word on a funny show, but a not so funny topic. *Euthanasia sounds like something having to do with youth, or kids, in Asia. But it's actually about the old and suffering across the world.* Euthanasia means 'easy death' in Greek. It's the practice of a medical doctor humanely ending the lives of those who want to end their suffering—like an elderly person with an incurable, incapacitating disease. *Euthanasia is not about kids in Asia but about the old and suffering across the world.* It is about if the old and suffering should have the right to an easy death, to euthanasia. What should the law be in the United States? And what are common arguments for and against it? Today, we're going to discuss and debate the ethics of euthanasia and what, if any, policy should be made about its practice."

LESSON

Information delivery
Close read

Provide students with two articles, one in favor of euthanasia, one opposed. In this circumstance, close reading can allow you to avoid bringing in your own opinion about a hot button topic and instead put the emphasis on common arguments around it.

<u>Priority points</u>
Priority points would be dependent on the texts students read.

ACTIVITY

<u>Metacognitive activity</u>
Modified Socratic seminar

<u>How it works</u>
Refer to the end of Chapter 6 on Activity for comprehensive detail on how a modified Socratic seminar works. Prepare Socratic prompts in advance.

Socratic prompt examples:
- If someone is suffering, do they have a right to choose a medically assisted, humane death?
- Should the American government legalize euthanasia?
- Is it immoral and cruel or moral and compassionate to allow those suffering to die painlessly?
- If there is a chance that a person's illness and suffering may improve, should they still have a legal right to euthanasia?
- Should a person's family members have a legal right to prevent them from receiving euthanasia?

After completing the Socratic seminar, ask students to share what they learned or if any of their opinions were changed from their discussions with classmates and why.

SUMMATION

<u>Making it personal and positive</u>
Euthanasia is a sensitive and heavy topic. Use the summation to help transition students' minds away from the specifics of the topic and to the broader concept of debating sensitive policy issues in general.

"Today we talked about a really difficult topic. I want to commend and thank you all for handling it with such maturity and being respectful of the exercise, the content, and each other. There are many adults out there who can't handle debating such topics with half the maturity you did today, so be proud of yourselves.

What we discussed today is but one of hundreds of really difficult policies being debated in America every day. Let's do a hot button topics brainstorm. To wrap up class, jot down three difficult policy debates going on today that you'd like to discuss in class. Also write down how you'd like to work with the topic—through another Socratic seminar, a concept map, or video curation. I'll tally them up. In the next class, we'll discuss the topic and activity you all mentioned most frequently. Thanks again, class, for such a productive and mature debate. I'm really impressed."

Exemplar 4

Subject: Science
Grade level: Elementary school
Topic: Weather vs. Climate
Standard: Use and share observations of local weather conditions to describe patterns over time.

ATTENTION

<u>Attention getter</u>
Game

<u>How it works</u>
Weather vs. climate dice game

Provide each student:
+ A dice
+ A key posted on the board as to what each number on the dice represents
+ A pre-made Google Sheet for students to log the numbers they roll

Key: Dice numbers represent the following weather:
1 = sunny
2 = rainy
3 = hot
4 = cold
5 = humid
6 = dry

A partial example of the Google Sheet follows. The numbers in the first column should be 1 through 30 to account for a full month.

Day of the Month	Dice Roll Number	Weather
1	5	Humid
2	4	Cold
3	1	Sunny
4	4	Cold
5	2	Rainy

Put students in pairs. Each rolls the dice and logs the results in their Google Sheet. After the first roll, provide students forty-five seconds each to debate who has the better weather in their imaginary town and why.

Once done, ask all students to complete and log twenty-nine more rolls, such that they have a month's worth of weather data for their imaginary towns.

TRANSITION

Bridge the known to unknown
Bridge the familiar concept of what the weather can be on a given day to the new concept of climate.

Script, with phrase that pays in italics
The key to this transition is using a mnemonic when saying "weather" and "climate." Speak them with exaggeration to convey their relationship to each other. To convey weather, reduce your voice to a whisper and rapidly say "weather." To convey climate, speak in a louder volume and really draw out the syllables when you say "CLIIIIIIMAAAAATE!"

"OK, what you have in your Google Sheet is a month's worth of data about *[rapid whisper] weather and [drawn out loudly] CLIIIIIIMAAAAATE!* That's right, *weather and CLIIIIIIMAAAAATE!* Which of those things do you think is short?"

Kids yell out "weather!"

"And which do you think is long?"

Kids yell out "climate!"

"That's right. *Weather* comes and goes in days, hours, sometimes even minutes. *CLIIIIIIMAAAATE!* is slow and happens over time. *CLIIIIIIMAAAATE!* is the pattern we can observe when we look at *weather* over time. *So we have weather, which is quick. And CLIIIIIIMAAAATE!, which is slow and over time.* How specifically can we tell the difference between *weather* and *CLIIIIIIMAAAATE?* And why does the difference between the two matter? How do they influence the decisions we make today and over the long term? Let's dive in."

LESSON

Information delivery
Lecture

Priority points
+ Weather is daily and local
+ Climate is over time and over a larger geographic area
+ Hazards come from changes in weather
+ Hazards come from changes in climate

Throughout or after the lecture, refer kids to their Google Docs to answer questions about their data to emphasize priority points and drive academic discussion. Examples of questions include:

+ Q: What was the weather on the 15th day in your fictional town? What kinds of decisions will you make because of this weather?
+ A: Invite kids to share their weather and report answers such as "wear sunscreen" for sunny weather or "drink a lot of water" for dry weather, and so on.

+ Q: What is the climate in your imaginary town, and how do you know?
+ A: Invite kids to answer and explain their rationale.

ACTIVITY

Metacognitive activity
Concept map and turn and talk

How it works
Have students choose any location on earth. Ask them to look up the last sixty days of weather in that location and log it on a Google Sheet. Analyzing this data, ask them to create a concept map in Popplet, MindMup, or Google Slides that addresses the following steps:

1) The focus question: What is this area's climate?
2) The key concepts: What are the key concepts, in rank order, that connect and relate to your main idea?
3) Connecting concepts: What are the cross-links that connect concepts in different areas of the map?

Once students have completed their concept masks, ask them to share and explain them with a neighbor.

SUMMATION

Making it personal and positive
"OK, class...we have *weather and CLIIIIIIMAAAATE!* If you could go on vacation anywhere in the world, which would you use to help you decide if it's an ideal vacation spot and why?"

Invite a few students to share their answers.

"So we all agree that when you decide to take a vacation, you should consider if the weather at the time will make it easy to relax on the beach all day, or spend the day hopping around to all the tourist spots, right? You don't want to be getting rained on at the beach, or freezing at the top of the Eiffel Tower in Paris, do you? And do you all know how you can take this vacation of your dreams? By working really hard in school so that you can get really great jobs as adults. If how you apply yourself to school on a given day is the *weather*, then the *CLIIIIIMAAAATE!* is your overall success in school and the opportunities you have as adults as a result. Today, your *weather* was sunny and pleasant—you worked hard and did great work."

Exemplar 5

Subject: Math
Grade level: Middle school
Topic: Order of operations
Standard: Use parentheses, brackets, or braces in numerical expressions, and evaluate expressions with these symbols.

ATTENTION

Attention getter
Challenge

How it works
Ask students how fast they can eat an "entire banana." Refer to Chapter 2 for the full script that Miss Curry used. As you prepare for the transition, continue to touch on the idea that order matters.

TRANSITION

<u>Bridge the known to unknown</u>
Bridge the familiar activity of eating a banana to the concept of order of operations by asking kids to consider where "eating" comes into all the steps that go into preparing to eat a banana and eating a banana.

<u>Script, with phrase that pays in italics</u>
Refer back to Chapter 4 for the full context on Miss Curry's transition.

"So do you think the *order in which you do this matters?* That's right, class. *Order matters.* That's why, today, we're going to learn all about order of operations and why it matters."

LESSON

<u>Information delivery</u>
Lecture

<u>Priority points</u>
+ The order in which you approach math problems matters.
+ Approaching them in the wrong order will yield the wrong answer.
+ The correct order is always PEMDAS. "Please excuse my dear aunt Sally" mnemonic.

Use problem solving teaching and break up its steps across the lesson and the activity.

Model for students how to use PEMDAS to solve math problems. As you demonstrate the process, ask students to direct your next steps. Explain your choices and thinking throughout.

ACTIVITY

<u>Metacognitive activity</u>
Remaining steps of problem-solving teaching

<u>How it works</u>
Ask students to solve a standard PEMDAS problem in a small group. Circulate the room to observe their work and academic discussion, providing intervention as needed. Then lead the class in a discussion of what they learned, where they struggled, and where they needed additional clarity and support.

Free students to solve a problem on their own, intentionally allowing them to productively struggle.

The problem: Ask students to create a math problem using parentheses where the answer reveals something personal about themselves. Examples include: how many siblings they have, how many times they've watched their favorite movie, the most pieces of pizza they've eaten in one sitting, how many hours of sleep they got last night, and so on. Once they've completed the work, give them thirty seconds to use PhotoMath to check their work. Have them write down the math problem on a piece of paper to hand to you. The paper should not have the answer of their names on it. But it should include what the answer represents (e.g., "this is how many siblings I have").

Collect all the math problems, shuffle them, and then redistribute them across the class. Ask students to solve the problems. Then ask each student to share their answer and what it represents, letting the class guess whose problem it was every time.

SUMMATION

<u>Making it personal and positive</u>
Thank students for creating such fun PEMDAS math questions and sharing something personal about themselves. Then prompt them to think about when in their lives order of operations shows up and matters. Invite them to share answers.

"These are all really great examples, thank you. Now what about how you all might order your homework tonight. Do you think you might do the most challenging homework first? Why?"

Invite kids to answer.

"It feels good to get challenging work out of the way, doesn't it? Did any of you have that experience today in class, when PEMDAS initially felt really hard but got easier with practice? What did it feel like for PEMDAS to crystallize and begin to make sense?"

Invite kids to share their thoughts.

"That's right, when we push through what's hard to discover we can understand challenging concepts, we gain confidence. And we gain new skills! Important ones, too. Skills that will show up outside of class. Just like order of operations, which shows up in our lives constantly. And here's the thing, class—order of operations is here to help. PEMDAS tells you how to tackle math problems. But the concept of order of operations tells you how to think through a problem or a series of tasks so that you tackle them in the most efficient and logical way possible. It helps us avoid wasted time and a lot of frustration. Order of operations is your friend! I encourage you to take it with you to help you figure out the best approach to any situation.

It's also your ticket to more complicated math problems. So I want you all to be really proud of yourselves today—you learned a new tool and skill that is going to help you advance to more challenging math problems. Class, I want you all to know you are capable of learning how to solve more challenging math problems.

This week, we'll continue using PEMDAS until we all have it down pat. Then, together, we'll begin even more exciting and tricky math problems—which I know you ALL are capable of handling. Great job today persevering through new and important information. See you tomorrow."

Exemplar 6

Subject: Literacy
Grade level: Elementary school
Topic: Fact vs. Opinion
Standard: Assess how point of view or purpose
shapes the content and style of a text

ATTENTION

Attention getter
Video mnemonic

How it works
Start class with a statement written on the board that is either fact or opinion. Make it provocative. An example: "I make the best spaghetti in the whole wide world."

Ask a student to read the sentence on the board aloud to the class. Without discussion, then play Flocabulary's "Fact and Opinion" video, which is a rap song with a video. The artist declares at the beginning of the song that he is the "best rapper in the world." Throughout, he repeats the chorus, which includes:

- "I need a fact. That's something I can prove."
- "I have an opinion. That's something I believe."

The video can be found at: https://www.flocabulary.com/unit/fact-and-opinion/

TRANSITION

<u>Bridge the known to unknown</u>
Bridge two familiar concepts—spaghetti and popular musical style, with a catchy and memorable chorus—to the concept of fact vs. opinion.

<u>Script, with phrase that pays in italics</u>
"So I have written on the board that 'I make the best spaghetti in the whole wide world.' Is this *a fact, something I can prove? Or an opinion, something I believe?*"

Let kids answer.

"Let's imagine this is a *fact, something I can prove.* What would I need to do or say to prove it?"

Discussion will reveal how difficult it would be to prove this because "proof" rests on people's own opinions and spaghetti preferences.

"So tell me, what's the best spaghetti you've ever had? Is it possible that you have a different *opinion, something you believe,* about who makes the best spaghetti in the world?"

Let kids share where they've had their favorite spaghetti and who made it.

"That's right. If everyone has a different *opinion, something they believe,* about the best spaghetti, how could it possibly be *a fact, something you can prove,* that I make the best spaghetti in the world? The difference between fact and opinion really matters, so let's understand why and how we can learn to identify an *opinion, something someone believes* and a *fact, something that you can prove.*"

LESSON

Information delivery
Lecture

Priority points
  - Facts can be proven
  - Facts are based on research and observation
  - Facts have power to influence
  - Opinions cannot be proven
  - Opinions vary from one person to the next
  - Opinions alone should carry less influence
  - We must look for clues that signal what is a fact and what is an opinion: language, evidence, references, etc.

ACTIVITY

Metacognitive activity
Jigsaw

How it works

Divide students into groups and provide each group with reading material. Be sure to provide half of the groups with material that is grounded in fact and half that is grounded in opinion. As students read and analyze their assigned content chunk individually, instruct them to list in a jigsaw graphic organizer what they deem as the most important points when it comes to discerning if their content chunk is fact or opinion.

Once this step is completed, students must teach their group mates what they learned from their reading, including whether they think their content was fact or opinion, and why. As students listen and learn, they list the most important points coming from the entire group in their graphic organizers. Next, students discuss and reach consensus about whether the full reading material was fact or opinion and justify their position. Finally, one or two members from each group present their conclusion to the class. You will reveal to each group if their assessment was correct. When it's not, help students understand where their thinking was off track and why.

SUMMATION

Making it personal and positive

"Awesome work today. And important work today. Being able to tell fact from opinion can be really hard. And sometimes people want to make you believe that their opinions are facts. And sometimes people want to tell you that a fact is an opinion, when it really is a fact, something that can be proven. This can cause a lot of problems and make it hard to have healthy, useful discussion and debate.

What if I tried really, really hard to make you believe that it was a fact that I make the best spaghetti in the world? And what if you believed me without questioning if I'm right or without asking me for evidence?

Imagine that you are with your friends at lunch, and you tell them it is a fact that I make the best spaghetti in the whole world. Some might also believe what you say without asking for proof and go on to share this as a fact with others. Others might ask you to prove it. But you cannot prove this, because this is an opinion, something you believe. All you can do is say again and again that you are right, and that's a fact. Does this kind of approach allow for a discussion? For conversation? For debate?"

Let kids respond and discuss.

"That's right, it does not allow for debate or conversation. What matters is that we avoid telling people a fact is an opinion or an opinion is a fact. What matters is that we're honest about what we're saying. Now imagine that I tell you I have the opinion, the belief, that I make the best spaghetti in the world. Will this invite others to share their own opinions with me? Will it invite debate?"

Give kids a moment to respond.

"That's right, when opinions are correctly acknowledged to be opinions, everyone feels welcome to share their opinions, too. And when everyone in your conversation is sharing their opinions, then you have a great conversation going. You are learning from each other and sharing things about yourselves. This, class, is what is called a healthy and respectful debate. And it is only possible when speakers and listeners can identify and be honest about what is fact or opinion. Knowing fact from opinion is really important to healthy conversation. And it is really important to healthy groups and healthy societies. Today, you all participated in healthy, respectful conversation. If you remain honest about facts and opinions when you debate, you will do your part to keep an open, respectful debate."

Afterword

The first time I saw *Pulp Fiction*, it blew my mind. I'd never seen anything like it. The characters, with their bizarre or outlandish personalities, their strange lives and eccentric stories. The spasmodic narrative arc. The way multiple stories unfolded and intersected and collided, often in shocking gore that managed to somehow be darkly comedic at the same time. The rapid-fire dialogue about topics I'd never even heard of. And, yes, the f-bombs. I'd be lying if I said my twenty-year-old self didn't love the scandalous number of f-bombs dropped (an eye-popping 256!). It was a full-scale departure from what every movie I'd seen up to that point taught me to expect. It was one of the few times in my movie-watching life that I felt like I'd seen something novel.

Pulp Fiction did not follow Freytag's pyramid. Or the hero's journey. I don't think it followed any formula that was known at the time. But it worked. It engrossed and engaged me from the first seconds to the last. To this day, it still holds my attention and fascination.

Despite the fact that *Pulp Fiction* took an approach entirely new to me and most audiences, it did have all the essential components of good story. It had a beginning, a middle, and an end. It had character development and plotlines. It had conflict—all kinds of conflict! And it had a resolution, in only the way that its director Quentin Tarantino can bring a story to a close.

To say that Tarantino took creative liberties is an understatement. He broke the mold and created a new one. And he's been incredibly successful in this approach.

The point: Not every popular move, hit song, or absorbing story follows the most common creativity formulas. Some iterate upon an existing formula enough that it feels meaningfully distinct. Others break away entirely and blaze a new trail. The number of possible successful creativity formulas in this world is infinite, limited only by the number of humans walking Earth at a given time.

ATLAS is an engagement model that works. But it is *one* engagement model. It is not the *only* engagement formula out there. Nor should it be taken as scripture, despite the fact that I am a believer, as are many others who have become familiar with it.

But far more important than belief in a model is belief in yourself. Let *ATLAS* be a starting point. Let it be a teacher. As you get comfortable with it and see it pay its dividends in improved engagement and student outcomes, take liberties. Get creative, and then get even more creative. Try other approaches as you see fit. Merge them with mine or merge them with others. Make it your own.

> Far more important than belief in a model is belief in yourself.

Just remember this: Each *ATLAS* component has a kernel of truth. Just as Tarantino doesn't ignore the most essential demands of storytelling, you should not ignore the most essential demands of student engagement. As you experiment and grow, please always hold fast to the core takeaways of every component:

Attention: Get it in the first moments of class
Transition: Connect the known to the unknown
Lesson: Prioritize information
Activity: Make it metacognitive

Summation: Make it positive and personal

And, of course, always remember that you—and your experience, creativity, and wisdom—hold the same weight as your students' needs in the engagement equation.

From there, go out and do what works best for you and your kids. Take a page from Tarantino and break the mold. I'd just stop short of the f-bombs.

And spread the *ATLAS* word. The more engaged your students are in your classroom, the more engaged they will be in your colleagues' classrooms, and the more engaged they will be in school writ large. In turn, you will feel more fulfilled in your practice. The more teachers who feel fulfilled in their practice, the more positive your school culture will become. It is not an overstatement to say that, when students across a school are engaged in their learning, everyone wins.

References

Chapter 1

1. Glen P. Nimnicht, "Windows and School Design," *The Phi Delta Kappan*, Vol. 47, No. 6 (February, 1966), pp. 305-307.
2. "Glendon P. Nimnicht 2002 Humanitarian Award," World of Children, 2002, https://worldofchildren.org/honoree/glendon-nimnicht/.
3. Nimnicht, "Windows and School Design."
4. Nimnicht, "Windows and School Design."
5. Arnold J. Wilkins, "Fluorescent lighting in school could be harming your child's health and ability to read," *The Conversation* (November 28, 2019).
6. Wilkins, "Fluorescent lighting in school could be harming your child's health and ability to read."
7. Christopher Bergland, "Exposure to Natural Light Improves Workplace Performance," *Psychology Today* (June 5, 2013).
8. Kenneth J. Cooper, "Study Says Natural Classroom Lighting Can Aid Achievement," *The Washington Post* (November 26, 1999).
9. Gallup, *2016 Gallup Student Poll A Snapshot of Results and Findings*, 2017.
10. Robert Balfanz, Liza Herzog, and Douglas J. Mac Iver, "Preventing Student Disengagement and Keeping Students on the Graduation Path in Urban Middle-Grades Schools: Early Identification and Effective Interventions," *Educational Psychologist*, Vol. 42, No. 4 (2007), pp. 223-235.
11. American Psychological Association, *Facing the School Dropout Dilemma*, 2012.

12. American Psychological Association, *Facing the School Dropout Dilemma*.

13. Gallup, *2016 Gallup Student Poll A Snapshot of Results and Findings*.

14. Kathy Dyer, "Research proof points: Better student engagement improves student learning," *NWEA: The Education Blog* (September 17, 2015).

15. Tim Hodges, "School Engagement Is More Than Just Talk," Gallup (October 25, 2018).

16. Mike Schmoker, *Results Now: How We Can Achieve Unprecedented Improvements in Teaching and Learning* (Alexandria, VA: Association for Supervision & Curriculum Development, 2006).

17. Valerie J. Calderon and Daniela Yu, "Student Enthusiasm Falls as High School Graduation Nears," Gallup (June 1, 2017).

18. Valerie J. Calderon and Jeffrey M. Jones, "Superintendents Say Engagement, Hope Best Measures of Success," Gallup (September 28, 2018).

19. Valerie J. Calderon and Tim Hodges, "K-12 Leaders: Student Engagement, Hope Top Measures of a School," Gallup (January 6, 2016).

Chapter 2

1. *Merriam-Webster.com Dictionary*, s.v. "creativity," accessed July 17, 2021.

2. Fred Vogelstein, "And Then Steve Said, 'Let There Be an iPhone,'" *The New York Times* (October 4, 2013).

3. Richard Gray, "Nirvana's 'Smells like Teen Spirit' Is the Most Iconic Song Ever: Computer Scientist Reveals the Track Ticks All the Boxes Needed to Be a Hit," *DailyMail.com* (September 23, 2015).

4. Colin Morris, "What Makes a Hit: 60 Years of #1 Songs," Columbia Business School *Ideas and Insights*, accessed July 7, 2021.

5. Paul Ashwin and Debbie McVitty, "The Meanings of Student Engagement: Implications for Policies and Practices," *The European Higher Education Area* (Springer, 2015).

Chapter 3

1. Jo Craven McGinty, "Is Your Attention Span Shorter Than a Goldfish's?," *The Wall Street Journal* (February 17, 2017).

2. Jo Craven McGinty, "Is Your Attention Span Shorter Than a Goldfish's?"

3. Jo Craven McGinty, "Is Your Attention Span Shorter Than a Goldfish's?"

4. Karen Wilson and James H. Korn, "Attention during Lectures: Beyond Ten Minutes," *Teaching of Psychology*. Vol. 34, No. 2 (April, 2007), pp. 85-89.

5. Diane M. Bunce, Elizabeth A. Flens, and Kelly Y. Neiles, "How Long Can Students Pay Attention in Class? A Study of Student Attention Decline Using Clickers," *Journal of Chemical Education*, Vol. 87, No. 12 (October, 2010), pp. 1438–1443.

6. *Merriam-Webster.com Dictionary*, s.v. "attention," accessed July 30, 2021.

7. Chai M. Tyng, Hafeez U. Amin, Mohamad N. M. Saad, and Aamir S. Malik, "The Influences of Emotion on Learning and Memory," *Frontiers in Psychology*, Vol. 8 (August, 2017), p. 1454.

8. Derek Sivers, "Keep Your Goals to Yourself," TEDGlobal 2010. https://www.ted.com/talks/derek_sivers_keep_your_goals_to_yourself.

9. "Ali G Medical Ethics," YouTube, uploaded by bogow (Jun 10, 2008). https://www.youtube.com/watch?v=lTaZ4b6l6II.

10. Diane M. Bunce, Elizabeth A. Flens, and Kelly Y. Neiles, "How Long Can Students Pay Attention in Class? A Study of Student Attention Decline Using Clickers."

Chapter 4

1. Chai M. Tyng, Hafeez U. Amin, Mohamad N. M. Saad, and Aamir S. Malik, "The Influences of Emotion on Learning and Memory."

2. Jal Mehta and Sarah Fine, *In Search of Deeper Learning: The Quest to Remake the American High School* (Cambridge, MA: Harvard University Press, 2019), p. 12.

3. *Merriam-Webster.com Dictionary*, s.v. "schema," accessed September 4, 2021.

4. *Merriam-Webster.com Dictionary*, s.v. "schema."

5. Jal Mehta and Sarah Fine, *In Search of Deeper Learning: The Quest to Remake the American High School*, p. 12.

6. Derek Sivers, "Keep Your Goals to Yourself."

7. *Merriam-Webster.com Dictionary*, s.v. "anaphora," accessed September 7, 2021.

Chapter 5

1. A.R. Luria, *The Mind of a Mnemonist: A Little Book About a Vast Memory* (Cambridge, MA: Harvard University Press, 1968).
2. Blake A. Richards and Paul W. Frankland, "The Persistence and Transience of Memory," Neuron, Vol. 94, No. 6 (June, 2017), pp. 1071-1084.
3. Youki Terada, "Why Students Forget—and What You Can Do About It," *Edutopia* (September 20, 2017).
4. Jaap M.J. Murre and Joeri Dros, "Replication and Analysis of Ebbinghaus' Forgetting Curve," *PLoS One*, Vol 10, No. 7 (2015), pp 1-23.
5. The Mind Tools Content Team, "Ebbinghaus's Forgetting Curve: Why We Keep Forgetting and What We Can Do About It," *MindTools Blog*, https://www.mindtools.com/pages/article/forgetting-curve.htm.
6. Chai M. Tyng, Hafeez U. Amin, Mohamad N. M. Saad, and Aamir S. Malik, "The Influences of Emotion on Learning and Memory."

Chapter 6

1. Peter Reuell, "Study Shows Students in 'Active Learning' Classrooms Learn More Than They Think," *The Harvard Gazette* (September 4, 2019).
2. Louis Deslauriers, Logan S. McCarty, Kelly Miller, Kristina Callaghan, and Greg Kestin, "Measuring Actual Learning Versus Feeling of Learning in Response to Being Actively Engaged in the Classroom," *PNAS*, Vol. 116, No. 39 (September 2019).
3. Peter Reuell, "Study Shows Students in 'Active Learning' Classrooms Learn More Than They Think."
4. John Dewey, *Schools of To-Morrow*, Scholar's Choice Edition (February 2015).
5. *How People Learn: Brain, Mind, Experience, and School: Expanded Edition*, edited by John D. Bransford (Washington DC: National Academy Press, 2000).

6. John D. Bransford, *How People Learn: Brain, Mind, Experience, and School: Expanded Edition*, p. 12.

7. John D. Bransford, *How People Learn: Brain, Mind, Experience, and School: Expanded Edition*, p. 12.

8. John D. Bransford, *How People Learn: Brain, Mind, Experience, and School: Expanded Edition*, p. 12.

9. John D. Bransford, *How People Learn: Brain, Mind, Experience, and School: Expanded Edition*, p. 18.

10. John D. Bransford, *How People Learn: Brain, Mind, Experience, and School: Expanded Edition*, p. 14.

11. John D. Bransford, *How People Learn: Brain, Mind, Experience, and School: Expanded Edition*, p. 16.

12. John D. Bransford, *How People Learn: Brain, Mind, Experience, and School: Expanded Edition*, p. 18.

13. Scott Freeman, Sarah L. Eddy, Miles McDonough, Michelle K. Smith, Nnadozie Okoroafor, Hannah Jordt, Mary Pat Wenderoth, "Active learning increases student performance in science, engineering, and mathematics," *PNAS*, Vol. 111 (2014), pp. 8410–8415.

14. Jann Ingmire, "Learning by Doing Helps Students Perform Better in Science," *UChicago News* (April 29, 2015).

15. Cynthia J. Brame, "Active Learning," Vanderbilt University Center for Teaching (2016), accessed October 21, 2021 from https://cft.vanderbilt.edu/active-learning/.

16. Garvin Brod, "How Can We Make Active Learning Work in K–12 Education? Considering Prerequisites for a Successful Construction of Understanding," *Psychological Science in the Public Interest*, Vol. 22, No. 1, (April, 2021), pp. 1-7.

17. Garvin Brod, "How Can We Make Active Learning Work in K–12 Education? Considering Prerequisites for a Successful Construction of Understanding."

18. Yale Poorvu Center for Teaching and Learning, "Bloom's Taxonomy," accessed October 22, 2021 from https://poorvucenter.yale.edu/BloomsTaxonomy.

19. Elli J. Theobald, Mariah J. Hill, Elisa Tran, and Scott Freeman, "Active Learning Narrows Achievement Gaps for Underrepresented Students in Undergraduate Science, Technology, Engineering, and Math," PNAS, Vol. 117, No. 12 (March, 2020), pp. 6476-6483.

Chapter 7

1. Mary Helen Immordino-Yang, *Emotions, Learning, and the Brain: Exploring the Educational Implications of Affective Neuroscience*, (New York, NY: W.W. Norton & Company, 2016), p. 30.
2. Mary Helen Immordino-Yang, *Emotions, Learning, and the Brain: Exploring the Educational Implications of Affective Neuroscience*, p. 31.
3. Mary Helen Immordino-Yang, *Emotions, Learning, and the Brain: Exploring the Educational Implications of Affective Neuroscience*, p. 21.
4. Mary Helen Immordino-Yang, *Emotions, Learning, and the Brain: Exploring the Educational Implications of Affective Neuroscience*, p. 18.
5. Chai M. Tyng, Hafeez U. Amin, Mohamad N. M. Saad, and Aamir S. Malik, "The Influences of Emotion on Learning and Memory."
6. Mary Helen Immordino-Yang, *Emotions, Learning, and the Brain: Exploring the Educational Implications of Affective Neuroscience*, p. 21.
7. Antonia Peacocke and Jackson Kernion, "Two philosophers explain what Inside Out gets wrong about the mind," *Vox* (June 25, 2015).
8. Mary Helen Immordino-Yang, *Emotions, Learning, and the Brain: Exploring the Educational Implications of Affective Neuroscience*, p. 18.
9. Chai M. Tyng, Hafeez U. Amin, Mohamad N. M. Saad, and Aamir S. Malik, "The Influences of Emotion on Learning and Memory."
10. Chai M. Tyng, Hafeez U. Amin, Mohamad N. M. Saad, and Aamir S. Malik, "The Influences of Emotion on Learning and Memory."
11. Mary Helen Immordino-Yang, *Emotions, Learning, and the Brain: Exploring the Educational Implications of Affective Neuroscience*, p. 20.
12. Mary Helen Immordino-Yang, *Emotions, Learning, and the Brain: Exploring the Educational Implications of Affective Neuroscience*, p. 18.
13. Chai M. Tyng, Hafeez U. Amin, Mohamad N. M. Saad, and Aamir S. Malik, "The Influences of Emotion on Learning and Memory."

About the Author

Weston Kieschnick is considered one of the world's most recognizable and sought-after speakers and educational leaders. He is an award-winning teacher, best-selling author, TEDx speaker, coach, husband, and father. He is the author of *Bold School, Breaking Bold,* co-author of *The Learning Transformation: A Guide to Blended Learning for Administrators* and the creator and host of *Teaching Keating,* one of the most downloaded podcasts in the United States for educators and parents. Weston has worked in collaboration with innovative tech and publishing companies (Google, Houghton Mifflin Harcourt, Apple) to redefine teaching and learning in schools. As such, he's advised educators from every state in the US and more than 30 countries around the world. Districts where Mr. Kieschnick has designed content, implemented initiatives, and trained educational leaders have been recognized by the Learning Counsel as being among the top ten in the nation for their work in blended learning. You can find Weston's work published in EdWeek, EdTech Magazine, The Spark, and featured on TED, the 10-Minute Teacher, Teaching Tales, Kids Deserve It, and LeadUp Teach. Connect with Weston via Twitter (@Wes_Kieschnick), Instagram (westonkieschnick), LinkedIn, or via his website: WestonKieschnick.com.

More from ConnectEDD Publishing

Since 2015, ConnectEDD has worked to transform education by empowering educators to become better-equipped to teach, learn, and lead. What started as a small company designed to provide professional learning events for educators has grown to include a variety of services to help teachers and administrators address essential challenges. ConnectEDD offers instructional and leadership coaching, professional development workshops focusing on a variety of educational topics, a roster of nationally recognized educator associates who possess hands-on knowledge and experience, educational conferences custom-designed to meet the specific needs of schools, districts, and state/national organizations, and ongoing, personalized support, both virtually and onsite. In 2020, ConnectEDD expanded to include publishing services designed to provide busy educators with books and resources consisting of practical information on a wide variety of teaching, learning, and leadership topics. Please visit us online at connecteddpublishing.com or contact us at: info@connecteddpublishing.com

Recent Publications:

Live Your Excellence: Action Guide by Jimmy Casas

Culturize: Action Guide by Jimmy Casas

Daily Inspiration for Educators: Positive Thoughts for Every Day of the Year by Jimmy Casas

Eyes on Culture: Multiply Excellence in Your School by Emily Paschall

Pause. Breathe. Flourish. Living Your Best Life as an Educator by William D. Parker

L.E.A.R.N.E.R. Finding the True, Good, and Beautiful in Education by Marita Diffenbaugh

Educator Reflection Tips Volume II: Refining Our Practice by Jami Fowler-White

Handle With Care: Managing Difficult Situations in Schools with Dignity and Respect by Jimmy Casas and Joy Kelly

Disruptive Thinking: Preparing Learners for Their Future by Eric Sheninger

Permission to be Great: Increasing Engagement in Your School by Dan Butler

Daily Inspiration for Educators: Positive Thoughts for Every Day of the Year, Volume II by Jimmy Casas

The 6 Literacy Levers: Creating a Community of Readers by Brad Gustafson

Made in United States
North Haven, CT
29 March 2023

34723277R00115